PRAISE FOR *HEART MINDED*

"We suffer when we become separated from our deepest, truest nature. *Heart Minded* offers us guidance on the sacred journey home . . . helping us to awaken from our busy, never satisfied minds to the heartspace where love is always and already right here."

TARA BRACH
author of *Radical Acceptance*

"A relevant, practical guide, full of inspiration to help you clear the channel of your heart and follow your truth."

ELENA BROWER
bestselling author of *Practice You*

"Gentle and wise, Blondin's approach is characterized by the bedside manner of devoted midwife to your healing process. Like her voice, it is a soothing poultice for the weary-but-spirited seeker. *Heart Minded* will crack you open down the middle from page one. It is all at once a centering meditation, a practice, and an olive branch extended into the depths of your soul."

PIXIE LIGHTHORSE
author of *Prayers of Honoring*

"There is so much that can be said about this collection of work. It embodies a bold truth that encourages self-reflection. *Heart Minded* unleashes the inner magic of unfolding to bloom."

ALEXANDRA ELLE
author of *Neon Soul, Words from a Wanderer,*
and *Love in My Language*

"In a world fraught with separation, anxiety, and distraction, there can never be enough positive attention given, never enough prayer, never enough books about love. *Heart Minded* is the antidote, the great reminder, to be heart- and love-focused moment to precious moment. Raw, direct, and accessible, this book invites and instructs you, as Mary Oliver once advised, to 'love the soft animal of your body.' Sarah Blondin, with equal softness of voice and heart, says, in effect, yes, it's safe 'to step into the wisdom of your own sensitivity' with heart wide open (listen up, fellow men, this is not a book for women alone!). Here you will find healing, creativity, and bright awakening beyond your wildest dreams."

ALBERT FLYNN DESILVER
author of *Writing as a Path to Awakening*

"Seems the great 14th-century Persian mystic Hafiz may have written an endorsement for this book years ago. As a famous rendering of some of his verse by me goes:

*'How did the rose ever open its heart and give to the world
all of its beauty?*

*It felt the encouragement of light—of love—against its
being, otherwise one might remain too frightened.'*

*The heart, even on its better days, can be just one wing needed to fly.
The other wing—love from someone else, or from a beautiful creature,
or some synergy with a gorgeous mountain or sky—can cause your
spirit to awake, unfurl, give thanks, and know joy.*

Sarah Blondin and her love, and this beautiful book, can be a golden wing, I bet, to many. I hope this book helps the whole world to dance."

DANIEL LADINSKY
international bestselling poet and author

HEART
MINDED

HEART MINDED

HOW TO HOLD
YOURSELF
AND OTHERS
IN LOVE

SARAH BLONDIN

sounds true
BOULDER, COLORADO

Sounds True
Boulder, CO 80306

Published 2020

Book design by Beth Skelley
Book composition by Happenstance Type-O-Rama

"We Should Talk About This Problem" and "This Sky" by Hafiz, translated by
Daniel Ladinsky, from *I Heard God Laughing: Poems of Hope and Joy*. Translation
copyright © 1996, 2006 by Daniel Ladinsky. Reprinted by permission of Daniel
Ladinsky.

Printed in the United States

Library of Congress Cataloging-in-Publication Data
Names: Blondin, Sarah, author.
Title: Heart minded : how to hold yourself and others in love / Sarah
    Blondin.
Description: Boulder, CO : Sounds True, 2020.
Identifiers: LCCN 2019029165 (print) | LCCN 2019029166 (ebook) | ISBN
    9781683643418 (hardcover) | ISBN 9781683644040 (ebook)
Subjects: LCSH: Love. | Self-realization. | Meditation.
Classification: LCC BF575.L8 B5575 2020 (print) | LCC BF575.L8 (ebook) |
    DDC 158—dc23
LC record available at https://lccn.loc.gov/2019029165
LC ebook record available at https://lccn.loc.gov/2019029166

10 9 8 7 6 5 4 3 2 1

To my heart.

I am listening.

And, to my beloved, Derrick,

my witness and upholder.

With love and gratitude.

The moment you separated from your heart, the moment you closed, quieted, pushed away, turned from, disowned, lost sight of goodness, the exact moment you began to splinter from love, a part of you began doing everything in its power to bring you back.

Just as a mother who has lost her child will never tire of standing at the ocean's edge calling out her beloved's name, sending prayers for survival, blessings in bottles out to sea, she, your heart, began to do the same once you were set adrift.

You are never lost, dear one, for the moment you divided, your heart began doing everything in its power to bring you home.

A LETTER FROM THE UNIVERSE

CONTENTS

INTRODUCTION

For small creatures such as we, the vastness
is bearable only through love.
CARL SAGAN, *CONTACT*

We are all born as pure light, our very life sustained by the beating heart that is here to guide and inform us. But because life is imperfect, in our very first moments of being alive, we discovered that the needs of our hearts could not always be met. Pain and sorrow began to pool inside of us, and in our desperation not to feel this pain and to protect our tenderhearted nature, we abandoned the one place within us intended to be our safe-hold. We orphaned the part of us that flows with the current of life itself.

We turned away from our tender heart and entered the mind, neglecting to come back and care for this crucial and elemental aspect of our being. Imagine taking a wing off a monarch butterfly and expecting it to fly straight or removing the engine of a car and expecting it to run smoothly. We know neither of those things are possible, yet we expect ourselves to operate unimpaired without the engine that is our heart.

Without our heart to soothe, affirm, and comfort us, we become lost in tormented and twisted thoughts about who we are; we suffer from self-denial and aggressive internal criticism. Never satiated, always seeking, we scour the world outside of us for worth and meaning. Turning away from our heart was ultimately an act of violence against who we really are. In effect, we removed one of our wings.

The consequence of this is immense; this cutting off from our vital core, our compass and guide, our connection to source. When we detach from it, we are left with the persistent feeling of struggle. We feel like nomads, wandering through fields of fear and scarcity. Something within us feels lost, anesthetized, unable to find home, unable to rest. We may experience small doses of heartfelt joy and alignment, but we know there is something amiss. We know there is more to life.

I know this feeling well. I have been there—in that variously numbed/lost/fearful/constricted place. And I have found my way back. My hope is that this book will crack you open to the magnificent powers of your heart, helping you rediscover the breath of love within you. As you learn to reopen to and live from your heart, you can't really help but fall deeply in love with this life, your life. Your fears quiet, your body softens, your shields drop and you open, curiosity awakens, and you recognize what a gift it is to be the wildly feeling, vital, and alive human being you are.

If you have ever stopped to ask why your moments of feeling openhearted, compassionate, and generous are fleeting, why your connection with your own heart seems somehow labored, this book is for you. If you are curious why it often feels so challenging to offer yourself openly to others, or why in your turmoil you turn away from yourself and your heart, this book is for you.

I want you to know that you are not alone. I receive emails in the hundreds from people who have taken my courses and done my meditations, all of them expressing deep distress around their broken connection with their hearts. They long to be able to hold themselves and others in love. After studying the ways of the heart for many years now, I believe I can help guide you back to this place of unshakable, unreserved love.

My earliest memory of splintering from my heart is from when I was five years old. I remember deciding that my bed was the only safe place for me to be. I had no words to describe the pain that I sensed in the people around me, and I felt very alone. I was constantly overwhelmed and alarmed. In my innocence and naivete, I concluded that if I were to stay open to feeling this heartache, I would die. I resolved to become impervious.

Each time I left my room I would armor myself. I would decide not to feel anything at all, or to at least try to ignore what I was feeling. It seemed safer to move through life this way.

This is how the great abandonment from ourselves begins. At some point, something felt too big for us to feel and too scary for us to hold, and in our innocence, we decided to turn away from our deeply feeling core, and our hearts. We became like lost children without a mother, without a safe place to land.

I was, for the most part, a healthy, happy, and well-adjusted child. But my struggle—as the majority of our struggles are—was internal, on a psychological and emotional level. I could never shake the feeling that something was missing, that *I* was missing something. There was a dull ache in the pit of me. The older I got, the louder the ache became, and life started to feel cruel.

Anger, victimhood, and righteousness were my bread and water. (These behaviors are what I have come to know as the most telltale signs of someone who has grown distant from their heart.)

For most of my mid-twenties, I would wake each morning to floods of despair and hopelessness. I would spend many after-noons lying on the cold cement floor of my apartment, weeping with a soul sadness I had no idea how to hold. What I didn't realize then was that behind that ache was a heart calling me toward myself.

Everything I attempted to pursue felt empty and meaningless. I was working as an actress at the time, and after the highs of booking a job I would eventually come crashing down, feeling even more unfulfilled. I, like so many of us, depended entirely on the outside world to confirm my worth and fulfill my needs, not realizing that in the act of looking outside myself for love and validation, I was getting more and more distant from myself, more and more lost.

Naturally, I grew irritated, exhausted, and so very heartsick. Behind the veneer of a blessed and abundant life, I was restless and unsatisfied. This suffering took shape in the form of anger and depression, a haunting loneliness and desolation.

I spent years in this place of reactivity and rage before I realized that there was a river of pure love running through me. I didn't need validation from the outside; I needed to connect with my heart. With nothing working for me in the "real world," in the world outside of me, I had to start looking elsewhere. I had to engage with the unseen world of spirit.

Each afternoon, when I felt the sorrow come, instead of drowning in it, I would quietly pray and then become still. As I created space around my grief, I would feel a powerful surge drawing me into myself. Eventually, the voice of my heart began to eclipse the voice of my suffering. I started sensing seemingly random requests in insights and bursts: Talk to strangers. Ask them what makes them happy. Meditate. Explore inside yourself. And I followed through with each and every request, sensing the urgency and becoming disciplined in listening to the inner mystery instructing me.

I was coming back to the home I had left all those years ago as a frightened little girl, and slowly, moment by moment, I came closer and closer to my source of unconditional love and divinity—my heart. My pain pushed until a greater vision, a heart-led vision of myself, pulled.

In learning to meditate I saw that my agony was not caused by anything outside me. Now, when rage would arise in my thoughts, I would follow the sensation of pain and find it in *my* tissues, *my* body, in the tightening feeling around *my* throat. I was being choked, not by something outside of me, but from within. All this hurt and heartache I'd been living with, as it turns out, was under *my* ownership; the onus to change was on me.

This was the beginning of my journey of self-realization. I became determined to turn toward and care for my uncomfortable thoughts and fears and the stories I was telling myself about why things felt the way they did. I wanted to stop bracing against life and start living it.

Gradually, the inner shouting stopped. The anger quieted. I became intimate with the feelings that would sweep through me. I witnessed them, I named them, I held them as one would hold a frightened child. I sat and listened to each feeling and sensation and watched again and again how my loving attention transformed them from rigid and inflexible to soft and undefended.

This gentle process taught me that I had a sacred choice. I could choose how I wanted to live. I could choose love or pain. It was about addressing, not avoiding, my afflictions.

My life, in turn, became less muddy and dense. I freed up all that energy I was using in anger and victimhood and used it as momentum toward more joy and freedom. I watched in awe as my external reality shifted to match this new frequency of love I was generating. Now that I was no longer holding the people and circumstances in my life accountable for my well-being, my relationships began to ripen and grow sweet.

This type of mastery, I've come to believe, is what we are all starving for. What we are lonely for, what we are longing to know, is our own loving. We are longing to become heart minded—to override the busy mind and its instinct to protect so we can feel and experience, bloom and thrive, rest and receive.

In her book *Upstream: Selected Essays*, the poet Mary Oliver wrote, "Attention is the beginning of devotion." I know this to be true. In becoming attentive to my body, mind, and spirit, I fell in love with myself, in my entirety, and I became hopelessly devoted to forever exhuming the wisdom of my heart. This period of my life was just the fissure beginning to open, the sweetness on my tongue that sent me seeking to uncover more. My heart continues to this day to further break open, imbuing me with more love. The unfolding of my heart-led journey continues in the chapters to follow.

Each of us has unique reasons for shutting down our hearts and hiding the parts of ourselves we are ashamed of. We tuck wounds and vulnerabilities deep inside and make our bodies battlegrounds. We push down and away all the ways of being and feeling that we sense—or are explicitly told—are "unacceptable," and create rifts between the self we present to the world and what is really going on inside us. Everything we hide and suppress siphons energy we could be using to create a beautiful life, and blocks us from accessing joy and abundance, dulling and dimming the light of who we are.

If we continue to neglect this internal tangle of dishonored thoughts and feelings, we generate un-love and dis-ease within ourselves. The fragments accumulate and collect, distancing us from the force that was meant to guide and instruct us through life. The heart. Through this process of dissonance and disconnect, we enter the realm of the half awake and fall into a sleepy state of suffering that is full of confusion, unexplained

hopelessness, anxiousness, and existential angst. We push things deep and away in hopes of burying them, but that never works. We become hardened, but our suffering remains.

To discover the language and message of our heart, we need to take the time to look deep within ourselves. We must decide to excavate, to search for the tender parts of us we have abandoned and hidden away. We must look to welcome home the split-off and orphaned parts. This retrieval of the forsaken is where profound and beautiful soul making begins.

Our hearts house the essence of life and source. They are the well of divinity within us, which when aligned with, awakened, and re-connected to, will eradicate and heal, forgive and dispel, and reconcile and release each hurtful relationship and memory. Our hearts are the source of our inspiration to spread and stir love and goodness throughout the world. I would go so far as to say that if each of us were to choose to live in alignment with our hearts, the world would have no choice but to find peace. The earth would thrive. How could it not?

We may once have had very good reasons to guard our hearts; we had to protect ourselves from further hurt. But from the seat of awareness, there is not one good reason to continue doing so. We are not born this way. We had to learn to shut down, and by the good grace of life, we can unlearn it. We can learn to open back up to the force of love and joy that resides within us in every moment of every day.

If you want to live a heart-minded life, the decision is yours, dear one. It begins by making the choice to take just one small step toward yourself, instead of away. Start gently blowing on the wounded and scared parts of yourself as if they were hot coals. Stoke them with encouraging words. Cocoon them in love. Genuinely care for them. They need to be coaxed into coming out from protection and they need a life raft to hold

on to when traversing through the rough and choppy waters of the darkness.

Most importantly, *you* need tender, gentle, and constant encouragement to strengthen your resolve in keeping your heart open, especially when your finely tuned instincts to protect are activated. This book is built of practices that will do just that. You can read the book from front to back, or you can open it to any chapter and start reading. Each chapter is designed to be its own whole. Slow down and settle as you read. Soak up the contents as if by osmosis, with your whole body, mind, and heart. And don't just read it, live it. Learn what your heart wants you to know; find your antidotes to the hindrances around your heart. Practice. Use this book.

Welcome, dear one. Welcome.

SOME NOTES AND SUGGESTIONS BEFORE MOVING AHEAD

As you read *Heart Minded* you'll notice it is designed to help you recognize how you splintered off from your heart and how to reengage with it. The book then delves into how to remain heart minded in your relationships, so you can hold others in love as well. Every chapter looks at this basic idea from a new vantage point and context, with practices that build upon one another. As you engage with this book, your understanding will broaden. I designed it this way to help you open your heart a little at a time. Small, subtle changes that will add up to great shifts in how you feel and experience life.

I need to emphasize that this book is not for the "thinking mind." It is written to bypass the mind and touch the heart. However beautiful an instrument the mind is, it often overlooks and tramples the wisdom of the body and heart. We can't think our way back to our hearts; we have to feel our way there. So, keep careful watch to make sure the mind doesn't take over. Maybe it starts racing with questions or you notice you are rushing ahead in the book to find answers. This is the mind assuming dominance. To quiet the intellect, just take a deep breath and

sink back down and in, like a stone dropping into the soft center of your heart. Let all the voices drop away from your attention. Become empty and you will meet the sacred space of your heart.

I include guided meditations at the end of each chapter to help you access the heart. They are meant to be used repeatedly until you experience a shift in your consciousness and in the way your mind connects with your heart. Heart mindedness will arise naturally if you let it. It is important that you read the chapter and then listen to the audio versions of the meditations, which are available to you for free online at sarahblondin.com/heart-minded-meditations. The audio component will help you metabolize the material from a heart space.

Some of the meditations and practices may seem simplistic or even cliché. A voice inside you may say you have heard it all before. I urge you to try and quiet these voices of cynicism or sarcasm. These voices are defenses; they are our mind's clever way of protecting us from *feeling* and keeping us away from our hearts. I get a bit embarrassed with how elementary some of this work may seem, but I know that in my own life, when I override this judgment and interpretation and allow the words to penetrate, I can feel the internal shifts. I can feel myself expanding, feeling unburdened by worry, and opening into a gentler, more loving space. So, I encourage you to open yourself to the words I am about to share. Move into your body and let it show you how it feels when reading this book, how it feels when it stops reasoning and evaluating and instead begins recognizing its own heart.

As you begin working through this book, I encourage you to keep a journal. Going through the experience will be like going on an inner voyage, and writing about what you encounter and feel will be useful in making the changes stick. You won't want to let any realizations or shifts or discoveries slide by. You may

feel a sense of hope for the first time, or the first time in a long while. You may tap into a deep sense of connection with yourself or receive a message from your heart. If you don't record the experience, especially if it seems small or subtle, you might forget it and find yourself slipping back into old, shut-down patterns. Keeping a journal will help you stay open and observant and this in itself helps train the mind to be receptive to the goings-on of your heart.

Don't worry about how it comes out or if the words are perfect and clear; the only thing that matters is that you start opening to yourself without judgment and censorship. Just begin.

The other suggestion I'd like to make is that you take time to connect with nature every day (without the distraction of your phone, music, or any other device). Even if you live in the middle of a big city, do whatever you can manage. The intention of this work is to open to our feelings and heart, and nature facilitates this opening effortlessly. Whether you push your cheek against the smooth bark of an aspen tree for a few minutes, tend to your houseplants, place your palms against a patch of grass, roll a stone in your hand, or sprawl on your back under a cedar tree, it makes no difference. Just find a way to connect as deeply and sincerely as you can with the natural world.

Doing this will help to open the heart and quiet the mind. It will pull you out of your head and into a larger, more expansive, and harmonious perspective.

Throughout the book you will find "Letters from the Universe." These letters came to me when this book was just a whisper in my heart. They flowed quickly and consecutively in the form of a story told at the moment of your birth and meant to support you on your journey toward openness. I felt I was accessing a higher voice, a voice of great wisdom and guidance, and felt called to share in some way.

I have come to know this as the voice of the heart—not my heart, but the heart of the world—and it's available to each of us. When I become open enough to receive it, it's as if a compassionate and loving frequency is working through me and I experience an immediate feeling of healing and release. My wish is to share this resonance with you, so you too might experience this comfort and support.

And lastly, I want to explain what I mean when I use the term *suffering*. Many people find it to be a loaded word and recoil. If you have that response, if you find yourself thinking, *I'm not suffering, my life is full and good*, or *I have nothing to complain about*, I ask that you make space for the possibility. Try and allow the word to apply. No one is exempt from suffering. It is the ache we sometimes feel when we are alone at the end of the day. It is that difficult place of not knowing what you want to contribute to the world or of holding your newborn babe, filled with feelings of love and awe, but also worrying for its safekeeping. It is the shallow breath, the inability to embrace simplicity and solitude. It is the clutching or holding on and not knowing how to let go of something or someone. It is our worry and fear. Our overwork and reaching for the future. It is present for us every day we are alive, in both subtle and not so subtle ways.

Denying your suffering, even if just a small stitch in your heart, denies you the ability to comfort and approach the hard things we all go through and feel. It disallows your healing and holds you apart from your heart. Admitting to pain and suffering is not something to be squeamish about. Embrace this, your humanness.

If we truly wish to heal from having split off from our hearts, we mustn't be afraid to touch our vulnerability or insecurity or admit we are hurting. This is what helps the heart find its stride.

This journey, I must warn you, is not for those who want only to feel and speak of joy. It is for those who are willing to walk through the mire that has been holding you apart from this joy. This is a journey for anyone who longs to lift the veil and look with deep curiosity at what lies beneath, for those who are not afraid to face all aspects of their experience. It is for the brave, for those who long to reclaim their freedom and wholeness.

PART 1
LOVING OWNERSHIP

With great difficulty advancing by millimeters each year,
I carve a road out of rock. For millenniums my teeth have
wasted and my nails broken to get there, to the other side, to
the light and to the open air. And now that my hands bleed
and my teeth tremble, unsure in a cavity cracked by thirst
and dust, I pause and contemplate my work. I have spent
the second part of my life breaking stones, drilling the walls,
smashing the doors, removing the obstacles I placed between
the light and myself in the first part of my life.

OCTAVIO PAZ, *EAGLE OR SUN?*

In order to harmonize with our hearts, we need to reclaim and retrieve our feeling sensitivities. In part 1, our aim is to do just that. I'll help you work through certain defenses, conflicts, and issues that are blocking you from being heart minded. I will guide you through specific practices to help you work through these obstacles. The practices are simple, gentle, and deeply loving. Little by little, you will be setting in motion a powerful unfolding as you learn to live from the generous clarity of your heart.

1

AN INTRODUCTION
TO THE HEART

You already know what it feels like to be in your heart. Though you may feel disconnected from it and at times doubt yourself, some very primal part of you knows exactly what it is to be in the seat of your heart. No matter when you made the separation and began living from your head, you know what it is to be in your heart. You do. It is a feeling, not something easily described or put into words. So, I'll ask you to reflect for a moment: What do you know about how it *feels* to arrive in your heart? Get curious. Become porous and listen inside yourself for answers.

The heart is still very much alive and awake within us. And most often, all we need to do to awaken it is to become still and quiet and it will do the rest. When we draw our attention inward and focus on our heart center, it will calm and reassure us, often instantly.

With it comes a softening of our bodies. We let down our guard. We feel a renewal of trust in ourselves, others, and the unfolding of our journey.

Fear begins to fall away. We become more open and peaceful. Thoughts muffle and we begin to *feel*. We are no longer preoccupied by problems and are filled with a sense of ease. Space opens up within us. Solutions to challenges we may be facing start to reveal themselves without much effort; we fall into harmony with ourselves and our lives.

This may sound too good to be true, but this is exactly what happens when we invite and allow it.

When we inhabit the heart, we awaken to our aliveness. We spontaneously arrive like a bolt of lightning in the present moment, and all our arguments against ourselves and life go quiet. Goodness pushes up through the chaos of our internal world, and we feel lit from within by a light we had no idea was there.

At any time, no matter where you are, no matter what you are doing, you can touch this place in yourself and activate the benefits of the heart space.

It is that simple. It's about shifting and moving yourself into this place of love and acceptance, allowing yourself to be infused with grace.

If we look within, most of us can identify a vision we have, an image of who we want to become, an enhanced version of ourselves—something like You 2.0. This image is often kinder, more loving, openhearted, accepting, inspired, and creative; it's often less self-conscious and more gallant. This self doesn't succumb to fear, anger, or hardship and rises above everything with grace and ease. This vision we have in our mind's eye is what I consider to be the best representation of our heart-minded selves. It is the call of our heart.

Unfortunately, the problem with this fantasy image is that we tend to misuse it. It often becomes something we use to belittle ourselves rather than inspire ourselves. We measure who we are against this fantasy self and feel failure and incompetence when we should be grateful for being gifted this vision of a more loving and able self.

When we see this version as our potential, rather than a reminder of our shortcomings, we can use it as a way—a tool—to help us move in the direction of our light. We can use it to inspire and motivate us to make choices that bring us closer to embodying and personifying this ideation. With each heart-led choice, we move toward our idealized vision; we become more and more heart minded.

The unharnessed mind will keep trying to get in the way of our heart-centered, heart-minded self. Because the mind is fundamentally concerned with keeping us safe, it will keep trying to prevent us from making choices that open us up to the world. And so, we have to keep overriding the mind; we have to keep choosing the heart.

As one of my listeners so beautifully said: "We are all connected and capable of incredible things when we simply allow the flow of this connection, this Love, when we learn how important it is to think with our heart." And, as Bob Marley says in *Redemption Song* while quoting the great Marcus Garvey, "Emancipate yourself from mental slavery; none but ourselves can free our minds."

It's time we undo what stands in our way and unblock what is restricting the flow of our true nature.

2

MIND, MEET HEART

*How can we drop what we are holding on to,
if we do not first look for the hand that is
grasping so tightly?*

Have you ever noticed that you have two distinctly different personae and tend to vacillate between them?

One is very rigid and concerned with the outcome of everything. It worries and frets, its gaze mostly downcast. It doesn't rest easily, even keeps you up at night sometimes. It acts almost like a dog chasing its tail. It circles obsessively over every detail and unknowable outcome, chasing the same things in a constant repeated pattern. It is cunning, convincing, and tyrannical in nature. It is feverish and ungrounded. Changing, morphing, and flopping from one story or idea to the next. This is your unharnessed mind. The persona you take on when your mind is not connected to the compass of the heart.

For most of us, that's the dominant persona. But the other aspect of you, as if by some divine intervention, will from time to time slip past the censor of the mind and cheerfully take over your being with its boundless and uninhibited spirit. This personality doesn't worry. Its face is often lifted, looking in wonder at the shifting sky and swollen moon. Lips curled into a slight smile. It is fluid and flowing, as if it's on a river of unending joy. It acts like water and reflects light. You feel buoyant. This is your heart-centered self, your true self.

Because most of us moved into our mind long, long ago as a way of protecting our hearts, we now live most of our time in that rigid, concerned first persona. Without even realizing it, we allow our minds to stand between us and our true nature. We have no (conscious) idea how much our minds are acting as a defensive block against our soft and tender core, constantly at work trying to find ways to keep us from feeling, from hurt, from heartache. The price we are paying, however, is that we are also kept from accessing source.

Now, each time we feel vulnerable or tender, our mind intervenes, shooing us away from our feelings. Even when we are feeling joy, it stands worrying at the borders, ensuring our pleasure doesn't last. Until we can deal effectively with how our mind responds to our feelings and emotions, we will continue the cycle of rejecting our heart and our freedom.

This rejecting of the heart looks different for everyone. For some, it may mean they close themselves off entirely from loving anyone or hide in judgmental thoughts that create a buffer between themselves and the world. For others, it is manifested in bursts of hurtful anger or in convincing themselves that they are incapable of both feeling and loving. For me, it was revealed through patterns of depression and despairing thoughts. Instead of facing my pain, I would revert to believing I was powerless. These tendencies are symptoms of a mind not in alignment with the heart; they are symptoms of being stuck in a fearful mind that's repeating the same self-deprecating thoughts.

In order to be heart minded, we need to bring the heart and mind into harmony and partnership with one another. For this to happen, we have to train the mind not to fear and close off from the heart, and instead, serve our heart and implement its wishes. In order to do this, we have to undo our mind's association of feelings of the heart with hurt and harm. In situations that would ordinarily have us retreat or retaliate, we need to remain conscious of what's happening and choose to soften and lean into our heart's center. Each time we practice this softening, we send a new message to the mind that signals that we are safe, willing, and *wanting* to live in this more open, more sensitive way.

Over time, if we are resolute in our intention to step into our heart, our mind will become less rigid in its defenses against feelings and tenderness, and gradually we will become more heart centered.

Remember, we are not trying to pit the heart and mind against one another; we are trying to marry their aptitudes.

Perhaps it would help to spell out how I see their differences:

The mind attaches; the heart lets go.

The mind operates out of fear and distrust;
the heart operates on faith and ease.

The mind is frantic in its functioning; the
heart is slow, deliberate, and peaceful.

The mind thrives on and enjoys problem seeking
and solving; the heart thrives on acceptance of all
things and labels nothing as "wrong" or "right."

As an example, say you are having a conflict with someone you love. First, your mind attaches to the problem and frantically begins to collect evidence against the other person. Fear and distrust surge through your body. What is hurting and sore within you gets covered over with anger and reactivity. You create a wall of defense around this soreness by shutting out the other person or trying to punish them. No one gets heard.

The hurt is left unresolved and a chasm begins to open between you and your beloved. The mind gets justified in its defensiveness; the heart of both parties is ignored.

But let's say a conflict ignites between you and your loved one and instead of reacting, you choose to calm yourself. You let go of that frantic, panicked, needing-to-be-right part of you and take a deep breath. You bring your attention into your heart. Let's say you slow down and sit in front of the other person and look into their eyes. You listen, you let them be heard. Let's say you defend nothing and instead choose compassion and deep listening. You don't try to make the other person wrong, but genuinely try to understand. You speak the feelings of your heart. You admit you are hurting, but you do not blame; you soften and express your needs.

What happens then?

Your heart takes over. Your mind in turn comes to meet the heart and begins to work at coming up with loving solutions. Both people benefit and bloom. The relationship strengthens and the love deepens.

Or, as another example, let's say a wave of anxiety washes through you. You notice your mind begin to race and attach to fearful thoughts. The anxiety then morphs into panic, which courses through you and makes you feel like jumping out of your skin. You begin reaching for an escape, resorting to some form of substance or distraction that can act as a numbing balm.

What just happened? Because you avoided your distress, you are only slightly comforted. A part of you remains braced under the distraction, in fear of the next time this could happen. Your mind's instinct to protect and defend has been confirmed.

Your heart is neglected and still aching.

But let's say a wave of anxiety washes through you and instead of looking for an escape route, you go to a quiet room to confront the feeling. You let go of the notion that something is wrong and respond as if something very *right* is taking place. You know some part of you is calling out for your love and attention.

Let's say you close your eyes and open your heart to the bigness of the feeling. You create space around it simply by looking without resistance at its contours. You know the only antidote is self-love and hospitality. The mind stops racing away from the distress, which makes room for the heart to begin healing and soothing the body. Your mind learns a new route. You are gifted with courage and resilience.

The only difference between these scenarios was one simple choice: to remain a bystander as the mind continues to ignore the call of the body and heart or to *act* in ways that support leading from the heart, so the mind can follow.

The two can be wonderful allies if we let them.

As we become heart minded, we begin transforming our human experience from something out of our hands to something very much *in* them. We begin to cultivate joy instead of haphazardly stumbling upon it when we are willing.

Each moment, our bodies are counseling us to make choices that bring us closer to love. The wisdom of the heart and body is there for us, always, if we listen and let it lead.

So, we need to choose to act from the heart. Seems simple enough, right? But there are tremendous barriers stopping us from being able to do this.

Over a lifetime, we have built a huge resistance to surrendering our defenses. So huge, in fact, that we can't even see it. Or we refuse to.

My four-year-old son once said to me, "Mamma, peace never wants to go first." He was explaining to me his inner struggle in choosing his heart. This inner struggle is present within each of us, starting for most of us when we are as young as two years old. It is hard for us to be in peace, to choose peace, to live in the peace of the heart. Choosing peace requires more than just saying it; we have to learn how it *feels* to live this way.

But before this can happen, we have to tend to the many fractured and injured relationships we have with our body. When we heal the disharmony within, we are free to let go of our suffering and enter the door to our true and at-peace being-ness. When we learn how good it feels, it becomes increasingly easy to choose it.

We start the healing process with a practice I call *Mind, Meet Heart*, which brings the heart and mind into our loving awareness.

💙

PRACTICE Mind, Meet Heart

(Listen to this audio meditation at sarahblondin.com/heart-minded-meditations)

I want you to close your eyes for a moment and move into a state of calm receptivity. I am going to guide you through a short prayer to the mind. Even if you have access to the download, I'd suggest recording yourself reading this practice aloud — or simply read it aloud. I want you to hear these words as your own, allowing them to soak into your being.

Now, place one hand on your heart and another on your forehead; this makes a bridge between your heart and mind.

> Dear mind, I bow to you and honor your great powers and the tireless work you do for me. You are a part of me, and I love you. But I wish for you not to continue to look for the things that hurt me and hurt us.

We must stop repeating that which does not serve us. I choose to move into my undefended and fearless heart.

Mind, when you start producing thoughts that squelch joy, I ask that you stop and stand as a fortress of love for me, repeating not the negative story of self-protection, but the mantra that *love is all I need, am, and desire*. Please align with me in the tenderness of my being, always, in the soft animal of my heart's deep knowing.

Please do not look for my pain in hope to eradicate it, but instead, take what hurts and stop it from spinning in its orbit. You are my ally, my friend.

I love you, mind. We are here to help one another, and this is how you can better serve me. Please and thank you.

Now, take both your hands and place them on top of your heart. I want you to leave your mind behind now. You can do this by letting all your thoughts go for a moment. Let even your personhood go, your identity as mother, father, son, or daughter. Leave what you are proud of, what you can't forget, what you keep reliving. Leave it now. You can let these things go. Enter the empty, sacred space right here in front of you. Bend your head down slightly, as if bowing to your heart, and gently lean into your heart's center. Allow yourself to deeply rest in this position of surrender. Feel your heart open more fully with each moment you spend with it. Give it room for movement. Let it hold you. Notice that while there may be a lot going on for you, you too have this refuge of the heart. It is always ready and always willing to hold and support you. This heart of yours wants to give to you.

Listen now to this message from your heart:

May I remind you of my service to you. You may put down what is heavy and come to me when you feel most afraid, lost, or in need of love. I am here at your beck and call. Please do not work so hard at keeping me safe, for I can never be broken. Work to soften the walls built around me, and I will fill you with reward and relief. Whatever you are in need of, I will give you. There are no wars to be fought; there is nothing to run from, for my gift to you is to soothe these very things, to alleviate your burden. This is why I am here; this is my service and gift to you.

This is what your heart longs for you to know. If you allow it, if you invite it, and if you work through the fear and resistance standing in front of it, your own potent and loving heart will feed you.

Recognize, dear one, that your heart, mind, and spirit are breathing in this moment as one harmonious system. Understand your role as the creator. You, by your own conscious authority, can bring your body into unity.

Open your eyes now; notice any small sparks of relief beginning to glimmer within, the embers warm at your core. Feel your eyes wide open and the relief of realizing your agency. Rejoice, dear one, you are coming home.

3

WAKING TO GRACE

Maps will be placed on the tip of each of your fingers.

Your heart will beat as a drum, behind the ribs of your chest. Life will move like breath in and out of your lungs, rising and falling just like the tides of the ocean. A light shines for you, high above, both in times of light and in great darkness. The same light is within you, at your center.

You will be born into form but at some point in your life you will close and contract. In order for you to live a meaningful life, you will have to learn to reopen. This will not be an easy process. Find water and sky. Lie often with your back against the earth; it will always support you, no matter what rages around you. Choose love and things that create waves of warmth within. This will tenderize anything that has grown hard and will restore all systems to their full function.

As you do this, all will seem inconceivably vast. Trust the kindness found in the eyes of others, the sound of air passing through your lungs, and the push and pull of the tide. These things will help ground you in truth; anchor you to the land from which you came, your essence and earth.

Remember, if ever in doubt: open.

To open is to spread wide that which wants to hide, to pull apart tissues grown tight and listless, to reenter your heart. To open is to face the shadow that asks to be restored to light. Bring everything that is hurting you into the light of loving awareness—for to see is to heal. The longer you resist this truth, the longer you will wait to taste the sweet nectar of life.

Lastly, do not worry. Worry is a weight you must free yourself from. It is a weight that severs you from receiving grace and removes you from the ever-shifting current of life. Your breath and heartbeat are your anchors back to truth.

Follow the instructions of the wind and weather: let come and then let quiet.

This is the cycle and circle that is life. Be in grace. Be in love. Choose not to harden in the face of all you will encounter, but instead, choose all that will cause life to burst into bloom.

A LETTER FROM THE UNIVERSE

Alone, I toil,
in the graveyard of my mind
until some sword of light,
some blade of wing,
some song of word,
frees me from myself
and leaves me rippling
in the ocean of the heart.

Now that we have brought our mind and heart into relationship, we need to begin healing our relationship with grace. Grace is an invisible force of support. It is what saved me from the fear, depression, and self-deprecation that we all endure due to our initial splitting off from our hearts. By focusing on the silent presence of grace through my practice of meditation, I was able to come back into myself and my heart. Fine tuning my rapport with grace is what made me feel safe enough to heal.

We have to work at discovering this grace for ourselves, as it is not something we are ever taught.

What I wish someone had told me was that my first step, the first step we all must take in our life, needed to be inward. That the most important thing I could learn to do was to sit still and open—to open to what was inside of me—and that the rest would come more easily from there.

When I was lost and desperate for direction and support, I wish someone had told me that what I was really longing for was to meet myself. That nothing else would soothe me until I first came to touch my own divinity.

While no one may have taught me these things, a higher force was at work. Something reached out from deep inside me and pulled me inward. I call this something *grace*.

Grace also looked like Mr. Bennet, my eighth-grade English teacher, whose kindness warmed the cold, teal-tiled school hallways; whose love for words and story resonated so deeply in me that the thought of a meaningful life became possible. Grace looked like my four-year-old son saying, "Should we dance, Mamma?" when I was reeling in sorrow. It was the ink-black raven flying by my window daily as I endeavored to write this book.

Grace is a hand that reaches through the density of our lives, our heartache and struggle, and brushes the angst from our brow. It is disguised in people and poetry or in bursts of beauty that catch us off guard.

Grace cannot be seen. It is felt. It is that feeling of being overwhelmed by goodness. It comes like a great benevolent gust, making us agape at the sheer mercy being blown our way.

I most feel grace, however, as a deep, unwavering force at the core of everything—me, you, the universe—and it always seems to be working to pull us up and out from our current stuck-ness into something more truthful and more meaningful. It operates even when we are most in despair; ever so gently trying to shift our gaze and our awareness back to our heart. I didn't have to choose this; the choice was and is made for me every day that I am alive. Grace works tirelessly out of love and devotion in the name of all living things.

With or without our consent, grace is always at work, nudging us to explore our internal landscape. If we follow grace's call, we discover that underneath the knots and noise of our lives sits a loving presence, unaffected by what is happening on the outside—a universal current leading all of us to a state of acceptance and peace.

I like to picture this place of acceptance and love as our taproot. It shows us that no matter the circumstance, there is a force of unfathomable excellence and intelligence holding us. Even in our most gutted places, we are not just held, but uplifted, urged, encouraged, and shown the truth underneath all experience. No matter the size of our pain, there is a stillness and deeply loving force trying to lift us above it.

There are many reasons we have come to forget about our core grace. As soon as we are born, we start encountering things that startle us and push us back into hiding, making us wish we had never left the warmth of our mother's womb. We learn within the first few moments of life that the one who birthed us and who we are most attached to is capable of showing us both love and scorn. We learn that to breathe means we can also choke. We learn that moving in body means we can ache in body, too. We learn that seeing means we will confront both the beautiful and the hard.

While life is inherently kind and working to support us, early (and then subsequent) experiences caused us to believe otherwise, and then blocked us from remembering that there is love and kindness operating within and around us all the time. We gradually and without conscious awareness began to splinter off from our heart, which is our source and true nature.

There are various ways you can recognize the space that yawns between our source and us. It comes in many forms, feelings, and emotions; subtle frequencies felt throughout our hearts and bodies. Inertia, fear, doubt, worry, self-hate, anxiety, panic, listlessness, despair, and hopelessness—essentially anything that causes a constricted feeling anywhere within you and your field of perception—are manifestations of the separation between us and our source. These feelings signal that we have lost alignment with our true nature. They are indications that the self we operate from moment to moment has grown distant from the heart.

Most of us are feeling at least one of these emotions most of the time. There are few moments in our day when we feel free from these conditions of separation. But when we were young, we really did not know any better. With no one to instruct or encourage us to trust the mystery that is life, we took this huge and overwhelming world both around and within us and made it small, compact, and manageable. We did whatever we could to feel safe.

Without us realizing it, the very structure we built to make ourselves feel safe *prevented* us from feeling safe and open in our daily lives. Ironic, isn't it? The things we do to make ourselves feel secure and in control are often the very things that make us feel somehow threatened and at risk. We took the natural fluidity and effervescence of the life force and put a clamp on it, closing ourselves off from the fullness and infinite potential of life itself.

Because we were not taught to tap into our own source of grace and peace, most of us end up waiting in this uncomfortably contracted state for something to break us back open to the truth. The grace of life always finds a way to lead us to truth, often bringing us back to our hearts and bodies through an accident or mental or emotional breakdown.

I know how harsh that seems, that grace disguises itself in accidents or disaster.

And yet sometimes it will—not to cause you harm, but to help bring your being back into alignment with the truth of who you really are, with your immense life force. It comes to help break you free from your cage.

You will often hear people speak about dark moments in their lives as portals that, while not purposefully chosen, ended up opening them to the divine source within them. They will often speak of how these uncomfortable times were what led them to discovering higher levels of trust and love for life. One of my reasons for writing this book was to offer you that opportunity to discover this trust and love without all the extra suffering. We don't need to wait for illness or the rupture of a relationship or some other deep blow; we can choose to move back into grace *at any time*.

We can awaken grace now and discover within our body a temple of respite. We can choose to meet our bodies and our hearts with soft attention, thereby opening the gate and discovering the gentle embrace of the universe.

I received one of the most beautiful examples of grace in a letter from one of my listeners. She lives in a very small mountain town of two thousand people, and she told me that recently the community had been devastated by many suicides, premature deaths, and serious, life-threatening illnesses. Both she and one of her dear friends had lost five people in the last year, and collectively the community had recently seen at least twenty deaths.

After being "called on by spirit to feed all that is holy and alive," these two women had created a community dance company. In an effort to help metabolize the pain many were going through after the deaths, the women poured their hearts into the creative process of writing a dance offering of grief. They felt a deep need to make something beautiful from the pain and loss.

Eleven women banded together and performed a dance offering for the spirits who had passed on and for the community. They wove together with music and movement a piece I wrote called "Accepting Change" and created an evening of healing.

"We danced, we cried together, we held each other, and our community collectively exhaled and inhaled . . . we poured sweet honey into the cracks of the cavern of despair," she wrote.

She expressed that it was love that guided them into the darkness and love that gave them strength to hold the despair and heartbreak of those suffering the most. Because of their deep listening, they were guided by grace, by love, and by the universal heart into a place of profound healing. They endured what no one should endure, but came out on the other side more tender and more available to love and to being broken open. They were carved open by the light of grace.

This mystery we are living is leading us to our hearts. We are meant to embody our softness, to live without barricades around our tenderness.

If you have been reading along thus far, I trust you have already begun unclenching and opening to your divine life. You are tired of living under the weight of your restricted spirit, and something profoundly loving is trying to show you the way out, by way of the heart.

You can help this process along by learning to soften the body. By carving out space to feel into your physicality, you can wake up your feeling body and touch that omnipresent peace that holds us.

PRACTICE   Leaning into Grace
(Listen to this audio meditation at sarahblondin.com/heart-minded-meditations)

Close your eyes now. Find your breath. Let it connect you to your essence and life force. Let it stir and open an ancient memory of your belonging.

Now, let all of the noises and distractions around you and in your mind fall away and out of focus. Let everything soften in the space surrounding you. Let it blur into the background.

Tap into your breath again and find what remains. Find what is still here with you when all the noise has quieted.

This is your center.

This is where we carry the light we are born with and the light we dissolve into. This is where we are awake. This is home, where all fruitful life blooms and lives, where nothing can be influenced, touched, tarnished, or hurt.

I want to take a moment to tell you that you are here in this moment because your highest truth, your soul, is pulling you ever so gently into your own light.

I want to tell you that you are doing so well, dear one, at choosing what brings you more love. You are doing so well at listening for what your heart is asking of you.

Now, slowly turn toward your body with loving awareness.

Bring your mind into your heart. Focus your attention on its physical place in the body. See if you can feel its loving current. Notice how its vibration is trusting and comforting. What does your heart feel and look like when it is awake, when you are awake to it?

Notice as it acknowledges your attention when you connect with it. Notice how it ignites and becomes more vibrant in your engagement. Notice how it is speaking to you, reaching out to you.

Notice how your mind will do the same when you visit it with breath and awareness. What does your mind look and feel like when it is awake, when you are awake to it? With your attention held on the mind, feel how it relaxes, expands, and quiets. Notice how it stops working so hard at trying to solve your perceived problems. Notice how when you let go, it too lets go.

Feel how much tension is released from simply visiting these two parts of yourself. With conscious awareness, your body will relax into its natural rhythm.

Let go, dear one. Place your body, like the blush petal of a rose, into this current of peace. Hand yourself over. Recognize yourself not as your story, not as your past, not as the being you wish to become but as this fluid and spacious self.

You have been working so hard to get someplace. You have been pulling away from this source within you for so long. You may rest now. It's time you come home.

May I ask you what made you forget about grace, dear one?

What made you stop trusting?

May I ask you what made you forget?

You once knew so well that you were held. You once knew life was supporting you. You once knew magic, sweet one. What made you forget?

Now I'd like you to close your hand into a tight fist; squeeze it shut. This is what it is to be hard. Notice how the blood in your hand is blocked from its proper flow because it is too constricted and misaligned.

If you hold that fist long enough, life will drain from your hand and it will go numb and listless. Now, slowly open your fist. Without any effort on your part, the blood rushes back to feed your hand with loving energy and life. Source floods back into you. It is effortless, easy, and limitless. It is full of grace.

You see, you are not separate from this source. You *are* this source. It is always there to serve and support you. It's up to you to decide whether you will close in fear and protection or let life take care of you in all the ways it always has and always will.

Every part of your body will let go if you pay loving attention to it. The energy of grace, which lives inside your body, will speak to you not in words, but in tender, life-affirming vibrations. It will thank you for not holding yourself hostage and will show you that no matter how hard you fight and contain and control, life is there working in your favor. There is a current of life that is steadily, beautifully alive and well under the weight you carry. It's asking, willing, and ready for you to trust your experience, trust your intrinsic nature, trust your heartbeat, and trust the benevolent language of your spirit.

There is a force within and around you that is continually holding you. We must find the same trust for this force as we have for our breathing lungs and pumping heart. The energy that takes care of our body is the same energy that takes care of our spirit. There is no separation. We are supported both in body and in spirit; we are just as sustained in the external realms as we are in our physical body. All is in our favor; all is taking care of our needs.

Let us come to know this energy of grace as truth. Let us come to know this as home. Let us come to know this as the root of healing and the ground we operate from as we move through our lives. There is nothing more gracious to know and understand than the kindness operating underneath it all, the kindness operating within you, the kindness that is life.

Open your eyes and please remember as you move through your day that all doubt and fear act as a closed fist, cutting you off from source. You always have a choice, dear one, to lean into grace instead. It rides on your breath, and is always with you.

4

RETRIEVAL OF OUR SENSITIVITY

You were born thin-skinned, as soft as milk. Still tied to the moon and starlight.

Built into the fibers of your body is an intricate system of sensitivity. This system is governed by love and kindness. Therefore, you, as a human being, are governed by these same virtues.

Because of this system, you are able to see and sense all incongruent, hurtful transactions between souls. Your ability to feel and see this discord is intended to support all human life. It is intended to help you strive toward actions of love and to help in healing the apparent disharmony you perceive.

It will be very troubling and intense as you learn to interpret the language of your body and sensitivities. You will be inundated with subtle frequencies of hurt and will see many people who are not living in alignment with love and kindness. This will be very frightening, as the umbilical cord to your intrinsic nature is still very much intact. Those around you are no different; they have just forgotten their mother tongue and have suffered a disconnect and dissonance with their feeling bodies.

All of this happened because feeling is seen in our culture as weakness, vulnerability, and frailty.

In an attempt to protect yourself from feeling the pain and disconnect of the world and of others, you too will begin closing yourself off from your innate sensitivities. In the misconstruing of your greatest strength, you will suffer a heavy poverty of self-love, feel shame, and experience dissonance from your truth. You will then begin the part of your journey where you will vacillate between your deeply rooted nature and the dark, sleeping, fearful unconscious.

You will meet very few people who know how to help you listen to your sensitivities. Therefore, you must be very careful to not let these parts of you go to sleep or be scared into hiding for too long. There will be signs and signals that will help you honor your native wisdom: keep your eyes and heart open to all that teaches and inspires love and acceptance.

Do not be disheartened by the unpreventable closing off from the foremost part of you. You can learn to reopen by continuing to expose your nerves and heart to the air. Do not shut these things away, for that is the surest way to harden a soul that was intended to be soft.

> Your sensitivities are your greatest gift. Be with them without the notion of frailty or weakness. If you do this, it will save you from becoming numb and moor you to your original blueprint.
>
> **A LETTER FROM THE UNIVERSE**

The body brings antidote
to swollen sting,
to mighty blow.
Do not be afraid
to drink in
the medicine
of your being.

My youngest son is extremely sensitive to harsh tones and angry voices or sounds. When he was just a few months old, he would wail as if badly injured any time I got frustrated or my energy shifted slightly toward anger. I had to be very careful not to upset his little heart. It frightened him so deeply. But I am human, and I could not always remember to be careful. Sometimes I still forget how to be soft and tender with both my own life and my children's.

Now that he has grown up a bit and has gotten used to the way things sometimes are, when I yell or get upset, he handles it differently. He has built a tolerance for pain. A tolerance for unkindness and upset. While this seems natural, it points to the fact that we each develop a shield to protect our sensitive selves from the pain and heartache around us. We all learn in our own way how to desensitize ourselves. This desensitizing is how we begin growing away from our feelings and hearts. At some point, we had to adjust and adapt to the environment we were born into. We had to ignore and suppress how we felt. In order to get used to pain, we had to grow hard and detach from our hearts.

But this is not how we started out or who we are.

We need to bring our loving awareness to the mending and healing of our sensitivities. We need to unlearn our desensitization in order to feel whole and well again.

There is a lot of pain in this world that is built up and carried in our bodies. It then leaks out in different ways and frequencies. Spiritual teacher and author Eckhart Tolle says we each carry within us a "pain body." This "body" is an accumulation of the emotional pain that you've experienced, which leaves behind a residue of pain that lives on in you. He explains that we can sense the pain body of others, too, and in some cases, our parents are even capable of transferring their personal pain into us.

I believe that when I was very young I could sense the pain body of each person. I think we are all aware of the apparent discord, brokenness, and contradictions that assault us every day—that cause us to recoil and shut off from the heart because it is responsible for feeling these things. It was that pain I could acutely feel when I was a little girl. It was that pain I was trying so hard not to feel. In order to cope, I developed a tolerance for pain in my own way, just as my youngest son is doing now. When I was feeling overwhelmed or frightened, I would sing and dance quietly, to myself, flitting around the room in an almost oblivious state. I was trying to spin myself a world where I couldn't feel the pain of others. But without knowing or intending, this dissonance, this not wanting to feel my feelings was forcing my heart to sleep. It was then that I began living in what hurt instead of living in my heart.

I hold remarkably few memories from my early life other than a general one of feeling adrift in a sea of people's pain and the unhappy undertow of the world around me. My sensitivity could not be addressed. My body translated my sensitivity as sickness. In kindergarten, I could barely make it through an entire day of school without needing to go home because I was feeling sick. I see now it was my way of withdrawing from the world. It was an attempt to comfort and soothe my exhausted and overstimulated body.

My parents were beside themselves and at a loss for how to help me. No one, including myself, really knew what was going on with me. I couldn't find the words for the internal struggle. Only now am I able to decipher and identify what the younger me was going through.

Why was there so much pain and unkindness? Why were people saying one thing and acting another way? Why was everyone living in so much fear? Why was my heart almost constantly braced?

The conditions felt too unhealthy for such a tender bud to grow. Doctors, ill-equipped to interpret the language of the soul, diagnosed me as lactose intolerant with irritable bowel, prescribing medication in hopes of relieving me of this burden. I could only manage to comfort myself by escaping into my fluttery state of song and dance or retreating to the safety of my bedroom. I took my brilliant acuity, my deeply feeling nature, and pushed it into the shadows.

My mother feared my fits of "sickness." In her struggle to hold and honor my overwhelm, she did as I'm assuming her mother had done when she had expressed her attunement and sensitivity as a little girl: she reacted in anger and frustration.

Without either of us intending it, her irritated response taught me to fear both what I was sensing and myself.

Every time I felt pain and unkindness in the world around me, I felt a tremendous rising of fear. With each intuitive hit, I came to fear more and more what was coming to the surface. Instead of nurturing the situation and myself from my compassionate heart space, I turned away, tuned out, and shut down. Like an overheating system, I combusted with unprocessed emotion and forced a very important part of who I was to go numb.

Every time I left my body in order to cope, I abandoned the wisdom of my own sensitivity, a sensitivity every person alive shares. Like a flower without water or sun, my feeling acuity weakened and began to wilt, while my muscles of fear, skepticism, and distrust grew stronger.

As humans, we tend to avoid what we do not understand. We fear what feels foreign and insurmountable, the unseen and the unknowable. We fear our sensitivities because we have no way to decode and understand them. As we push off and away from ourselves and source, we, in our dissonance, create waves of disharmony throughout the world and in our own bodies.

But all is not lost. As we have seen, we can learn to nurture our brilliance, tuning in to what is most needed in any given situation. If we sense pain or disharmony, we have the power to bring forward our compassion. Instead of operating from fear, we can slowly work toward healing. We can hold ourselves, the world, and each person in it from the seat of our wise, intuitive self.

In *The Collected Works of Mahatma Gandhi*, Gandhi perfectly articulated this concept when he said: "We but mirror the world. All the tendencies present in the outer world are to be found in the world of our body. If we could change ourselves, the tendencies in the world would also change. As a man changes his own nature, so does the attitude of the world change towards him. This is the divine mystery supreme. A wonderful thing it is and the source of our happiness. We need not wait to see what others do."

Of course, when I was young I didn't have the words I have now, nor the understanding, but looking back at that sick and scared little girl, I see that she was searching for a hand to guide and hold hers in the ocean of the world's heartache; one that could help her maintain and nurture her sensitivity. She was looking for someone to show her that if rooted from a place of love, her feelings could help create a different earth.

The world would have been a very different place for me had someone been able to explain the confusion and malaise we are born into. If they'd been able to explain that I was not wrong to feel the pain of it, but rather exactly right. I was not weak, I was not sick. I was feeling my power and wisdom travel through me with ferocity, trying to bring forth healing.

It would have been very different had someone told me that the voice of guidance I was looking for was the voice of my heart. That it could show me how to breathe through the discomfort I sensed; that all the power, authority, and compassion I would ever need were right here inside me.

A young man who, similar to me, suffered most of his life from various "unknown medical conditions" once wrote to me. He had found himself on a full-time medical leave because his body had had "enough of my suppressing and failing to realize the emotional damage that I found myself in."

At a loss for how to process the traumas he had faced in his life, he learned to turn inward and began a meditation practice. With the help of his doctor and my guided meditations, he was able to move through his pain and into his heart. "Daily, I came to cope. Cope turned into living. Before I knew it, I was headed back to work." Through his practice of honesty and self-care he found himself again, and learned "most importantly, how to love again."

He overcame the illnesses that came from what he calls "my years of being disconnected." He overcame the dis-ease in his body by undoing his desensitization. He found wellness by embracing, not abandoning, himself. He let his pain lead him to his liberation.

Having lived in this world awhile, and having spoken to so many others who have experienced a similar pain of disconnection, I know that we can restore our system to balance by reviving our sensitive natures. By reclaiming our inherent powers to see pain and empathize, we can stay in the heart space when it would otherwise threaten to close. We can come to understand that *we* are all the support we need.

The genius behind all of this is that our sensitivities never really went anywhere. They are built into us, and they are always operating, even when we are at our most fraught. We never fully became insensitive because our body is built of truth. Attunement and compassion are part of us, never entirely lost or irretrievable. Our innate sensitivity stands beside the pain, waiting for us to choose, to remember who we are.

PRACTICE   Seed of Sensitive Softness

(Listen to this audio meditation at sarahblondin.com/heart-minded-meditations)

Close your eyes now. Feel your breathing, the hum of energy in your body. Trace your fingers over the palm of your open hand. Begin to awaken your gift of feeling, the sense that is touch. See how it is bringing you closer to feeling your aliveness.

Remember, you are meant to inhabit all of your feeling, all of your knowing, all of your wisdom. Let it be lived; allow all of you its breath.

Placing your hand on your heart, repeat the words *I see you; I hear you; I love you.*

With these words, we shift into the territory of the heart and shine the light of our presence on what has most often been starved and neglected: our love for who we are.

Do not let shame come with this discovery, for to fall into shame is to fall victim to the voice of sabotage, and that will stop you from moving forward. Love and compassion for yourself is what is most needed now and always. You were not wrong for not loving or listening to your heart or body's wisdom. You simply were not taught to do it.

Here are some truths I'd like to remind you of:

> You are the soft earth that sprouts new life. You are malleable;
> not stone, but petal soft. You are warm to the touch and loving, so
> capable of loving.

> You are sensitive. You hear and sense what is beyond seeing. You
> sense what is said between others, even without words. You feel
> the aching of a heart beyond the shouting. You are supremely
> sensitive.

> Let me remind you how deeply you are able to feel — the power of
> the sometimes-subtle and sometimes-searing feeling is your gift. It
> is your guide. Give yourself permission to feel what asks to be felt.
> With your loving awareness, it will lift instead of lodge.

> You need not be so strong; it is in softening that you will find
> freedom. Do not defend yourself but learn instead how to stand in
> your openness.

> Under all fear, numbness, anger, avoidance, and trepidation; under
> all chaos, distrust, despair, inertia, and contempt; under each of

these symptoms of disconnect is something pure, something you have been protecting. This, dear one, is that seed of your sensitive self. You can reach this pure self with your own presence.

Now, let a soft light be brought into the dark belly of you and feel for a nerve. Dropping deeply into the heart and stomach, feel for a small pang, ache, or raw tender edge. If you sense even the smallest feeling of sorrowfulness … this is your seed. This is what has been abandoned. If nothing comes up for you, just rest in the space of your heart, with the intention of softening.

Try your best not to deny yourself this moment of true intimacy. Be available and affectionate toward yourself. There is great healing in this recognition of and touching into your sensitive edge. It is best to let yourself feel your own ache. There is no homecoming to our hearts without feeling all of what is here, without mourning the disconnection that we have each suffered.

We are often grateful for the gift of sight. Grateful for the gift of hearing, for the ability to taste, and to touch. But are we grateful to feel? Are we grateful for the sense of feeling?

Not long ago you knew how to dance when your heart wanted to. Not long ago you knew how to sing when the sky opened and the sun asked you to. Not long ago you knew how to cry when the water would rise within you. Not long ago you were but a seed, happy to be blown by the wind. Not long ago, dear one, you were alive to all your being senses. Not long ago, dear one, you knew how to be as you were. As you are. Remember you, as a young bud, reaching for the sun. As a small babe, open wide in the arms of love. Remember you, dear one.

Now, speaking to whatever has been opened and revealed, say:

> *I will not forget you. I will not abandon you, my sweet heart. I will meet you daily. I will come home to tend lovingly to my sensitive seed. I am here now, aware of you and you of me. I will not forget you. I love you and I am here.*

Breathe in receptivity and communion. Let yourself be fed. Feel the light opening anything grown hard and closed. This is how we open fearlessly and lovingly to a deeper listening and love. Remember this: when you are hard, you have simply forgotten to tend to the sensitive seed of your softness.

Opening your eyes now, try and hold this softness in your day. Hold in this softness when you are with others, when reaction and walls come between you. Hold in this softness, dear one. This is how you will awaken your intuitive powers of healing; this is how you will disarm yourself and the sensitivity in others.

Try to begin each day and end each day with your own touch. A homecoming; a gratitude, an exhausted delight in all you were blessed to feel, all that squeezed you in its loving grasp — all of it. This is why you are here; this is why you are here. Be soft enough and available enough, so you can feel it.

5

RETRIEVAL OF OUR
FEELING BODY

Before we can speak, we cry to express our discomfort. If something hurts, scares, overwhelms, or is not kind or loving, our bodies create a reaction that signals to our caregiver that we feel distress and need help in coming back to peace. As we grow into our independence, we still experience overwhelming feelings, but rarely are we taught discerning steps to self-soothe or transcend the upset. Instead of getting help to come back to harmony, as we (hopefully) did when we were babies, we most likely encounter a hurtful or confusing reaction, like being lobbed into our room until we learn to "control ourselves," or suppressing the emotions and feelings that came to the surface. No tools, no discussion, no illumination of what was going on, no understanding, and no language to help ease our inevitable storms.

Because they didn't know how, our parents provided little help at discerning the wisdom of our feelings (and their parents likely did the same).

With harsh reactions like these, it's no wonder most of us tried to cut the cord on our feeling intelligence. We learned through these uncaring experiences that homeostasis required doing the opposite of what our feelings *actually* needed. We learned to pull ourselves closed instead of remaining open. We learned to internalize instead of verbalize; to ignore instead of liberate; to shame instead of translate; to berate instead of acknowledge and name; to avoid and abandon instead of rerouting back to love.

Because of this backward understanding, we learned that feeling was weakness and vulnerability was frailty. As a result, our brains did not create healthy pathways to higher levels of consciousness. (This is quite literally true.) We learned that to express our feelings was to suffer alienation and at times punishment, so we taught our minds to respond in retaliation against any further "outbursts" of sensitivity. When overwhelming feelings arose, we divided in two, telling our brain to ignore the signs and signals of our emotional bodies and hearts. As a result, we were left to steep in a tremendous amount of undigested pathos and misunderstandings of self. We created closed loops of thought, avoiding the very things we would need to look at in order to be lifted to higher ground. We began to live with a great, subconscious fear of relationships, feelings, and safety.

After my four-year-old has a blowout with his little brother, I will usually carry him to his room as he cries. I have to work against every reflex I have not to lock him away until he calms himself down. Instead, I calm myself down, pull him onto his back where he cannot physically hide and curl away like he wants to, and we breathe together. We move into our bodies, we look into each other's eyes, and we become present as best we can. And every time, the first thing he says, without coaxing from me is, "I'm sorry." I respond with a heartfelt sorry, too, and we hold each other for a moment before diving into the problem-solving part of our talk.

I'm working on teaching him (and myself) that we are each made of love. When we do things not from love, like hit or steal or scream at one another, it's because we have temporarily forgotten who we are. No one means to get angry or hurt another person. All can be forgiven if we arrive back to our truth and our loving selves. He's only four years old, but I can see that he understands this concept. I see him relieved by my guidance and my support, by my not shutting him in his room alone to try and make sense of it all. I see him relieved to arrive back in his heart.

If I were to leave my son, as I admit I have at times, he would physically coil into a ball and shut his feelings, his heart, and his emotions away and out of sight. His pain would harden inside of him and begin to bog down his little body. The "time-outs" we are accustomed to giving our children when they are stuck in some form of distress would be so much better if used as a "time-in." A time where we turn inward together to work at undoing the confusion and to lay flat the corners of resistance, so we don't build so many walls. A time where we learn it is safe to live and to love.

I know that if I don't spend the time to talk us both down from our reactive selves, both of us will be left stunted in our growth.

When we respond in fear and fury, we shut the door to the pathway leading to greater love and compassion.

We expect both our children and ourselves to be well adapted and healthy cells of light, but how can we be that when we continue to ignore our sensitivities and thus perpetuate the disharmony between mind, body, and heart? How can we be healthy, beaming cells of light if we keep censoring what we feel?

6

HOW TO RETRIEVE FEELING

The "intricate system of sensitivity" mentioned in the Letter from the Universe that led off chapter 4 is our inborn compass set on love and kindness. In our body's effort to heal the disharmony in us or in what we are facing, our heart either speaks and translates our experiences by radiating life-affirming frequencies and vibrations through the body or by seizing and contracting. We call these frequencies *feelings*.

When we are not in alignment with our heart, we create uncomfortable sensations in the body. This is the way our feeling intelligence speaks. This state of discomfort is not relieved until everything we are feeling has been acknowledged and then fed with love. If we do not understand this principle, we can stray very far into the dark side of our feeling bodies and become identified with what is aching within us. If we are not aware that these sensations and feelings need our compassionate attention before our body can resume its healthy functioning, we merge with the pain body and enter immense suffering.

In the case with my son, until I learned how to calm us both, we would momentarily become lost from origin, from love, from kindness. Our bodies would react with dreadful sensations of rage to signal our disconnect and then we had a choice to make: we could either continue choosing things that caused us to remain identified with the pain, by screaming and locking ourselves behind doors, *or* we could respond consciously to the pain caused by the hurtful feelings storming within us.

In calming and honoring each misunderstanding, we find our way back to our hearts, to forgiveness, to love.

Once we align with our sensitivities, we can use these places of conflict and feelings of pain not to fall deeper down the rabbit hole of suffering, but instead as a call back to truth. When we turn toward ourselves to acknowledge the feelings that are causing us to withdraw and shut down and give them room to speak, we can then more easily return to peace.

After a lifetime of ignoring our pain, most of us have developed deep ruts, but as we begin to deal with our issues upon impact—not later, but in the moment—we can avoid these ruts and find our way to smoother paths.

Sustained vulnerability is needed for this to work. If we do not allow ourselves to be soft and open, nothing can flow or move forward and out. Sustained vulnerability is a continued practice of remaining in the face of things that make us want to retreat.

If you maintain a conviction to become heart minded, you will find ways to disengage with the hurt and enter into a field of acceptance and love within yourself. You will learn to pull yourself into the open clearing and pour light over whatever it is that wants to retaliate against loving. You will choose to let your sensitivity instruct you to freedom.

These are not choices anyone else can or will make for you. They are yours. They are the very choices you were not told about at the beginning of your life, and the very reason you ended up so lost from source. If you choose to become heart minded, fear and pain won't go away, but now you'll have a means for letting them flow out after they flow in. They'll no longer have the chance to become lodged or held deep within.

PRACTICE   You Are Allowed

(Listen to this audio meditation at sarahblondin.com/heart-minded-meditations)

"You are allowed." No one said this to us. Fear came, upset boomed, things broke, we broke, we hurt, and we yelled in anguish to the world around us. When we felt our deepest heartache, no one said we were allowed to simply feel all of it. Instead we were taught to hide, deny, and abandon ourselves, to condemn the pain instead of comfort it. We ignored our feelings and hampered our body's inborn process of healing. No one knew any better.

But now we know that our bodies are here to speak to us. In our upset, our bodies are asking for loving attention, not abandonment. So, let's work on allowing our feeling intelligence its rightful place in our body. Let's give ourselves permission to thaw our frozen emotions and seeming fragility. Let's give vulnerability a throne and a voice. Let's give ourselves back to our self, listening to our needs and finding freedom by honoring our brilliant and intricate system of sensitivity.

Close your eyes, coming to feel your body breathing, to feel your aliveness. Look for the gentle current of grace running through your body.

Allow yourself to enter this grace. Allow yourself to become one with this grace. Becoming more and more available and receptive to your spirit, to your heart, to yourself.

Can you remember, dear one, when you stopped allowing yourself to feel? Can you remember when you began coping instead of living? Can you remember, dear one, what caused you to leave the seat of your heart?

Who told you it was not all right to be? Who told you that you were not allowed, sweet one?

This was an accident. All of this denying who we really are was an accident. Go back to yourself, as you were when you were young, as you were when you were just a new sprout of life. Reach out your hand to this tremendously vital and vibrant child that is you. That is you before you forgot. That is you before you left home.

You don't have to leave this self behind, dear one. Reach out your hand and bring yourself home. You are allowed to see, to feel, to express, to wonder, to relish, to live in abandon. You are allowed to be who you were born to be, to be as you were born.

Place both your hands over your heart, and begin opening to yourself, this moment, and these words:

> I am allowing the great currents of my feeling sensitivities to be a part of me, not apart from me. I am allowing the great wisdom of my brokenness and feelings of disconnect to help guide and instruct me to embrace my tender heart. I will not fear the fear within, or the wounds and memories of hurt. I will allow them their place and their voice.

> When pain comes, I will listen. I will make space to be the ear my wounds are most in need of. I will listen so that my distress has room to leave through the door of my presence.

> I am allowed to be in all of the ways I need, without shame or embarrassment. This is how I free myself from recycling my hurt.

When we let go of our resistance and shame and begin a dialogue with our feelings, we strengthen the muscle of our heart and develop a strong spine of compassion. In shifting our perspective to one of allowance and acceptance, we gradually begin fostering peace and love on the inside. It then leaks out into the world and those around us. This is the power of inner acceptance.

Please remember, dear one, to bend to the needs of expression and feeling that knock at the door of your heart. When something surfaces that demands your attention, take your hand to your heart. Gently bow your head toward it. Let all come as it asks. We need not fight against ourselves; we need only to allow and set free.

To be allowed — no matter our kicking and screaming, this is how we long to be loved. So, this, dear one, is how we learn to love first our own beings.

7

GIVE NAME

There is no greater defeat
than a soul that has grown hard and closed
under the weight of the unkind,
the weight of the unspoken,
the weight of the untruths
locked inside them
longing to be set free.

People often say that they don't know what they feel. They can't identify their feelings in the moment that they're happening and have no vocabulary for what they are going through. Just as our sensitivities have had very little nurturing, we have almost no language to use when we need it most. It's essential that we work at naming what we are experiencing because the more we learn to identify the constricting feelings in our bodies, the better equipped we are to catch pain before it attaches itself to us too deeply. In identifying it we grow awareness and in awareness we are able to choose freedom. That's why we're going to spend some time now taking a deep dive into the practice of naming our uncomfortable feelings as they come.

Do we not each long to have a name? Do we not each want to be seen, heard, honored, and loved? Do we not each want at least the chance to be exonerated from the place of darkness and shadow?

We all know these places of storm within us: uncomfortable restlessness in the body; addictive behaviors like overwork, over-eating, drinking, shopping, judgment, and gossip; too much screen time; an internal discourse of abuse and criticism; and fits of panic and fear. Our pain is disguised in these habits. The behaviors are not the problem; they are our attempt at creating a solution for a feeling we don't know how to hold and address.

When suffering, or escaping from our suffering by getting caught up in any of the habits listed above, we are ignoring the call for healing. These unhealthy and uncomfortable tendencies will begin to choke your life, and their grasp will not loosen until what has been veiled is unveiled, released, cried out, and spoken out loud. Painful feelings and memories arise not to dig them-selves deeper into you, but to wedge themselves loose. They are asking for their emancipation.

So, remember that each time discomfort visits, it is really asking: Are you ready to speak, to name and honor this part of you? Are you ready to hold and love yourself and so be restored?

There is no "right" or "wrong" way to approach your feelings. When hard emotions or memories surface, begin by opening the door and paying attention. Feelings disguise themselves as heat in the body; a quickening of the heart, a shortness in breath, a turning in the stomach, or at times, a constricting sensation in the throat. Our job, when these things arise, is to notice and touch these places with thoughtfulness. Be curious, concerned, caring, and nurturing, but, most importantly, lean in and *feel* them. If you can, try to name what is hidden within the sen-sation. Is it rage? Disappointment? You can even express entire sentences, like *No one hears me*, or *I'm feeling lost and confused, empty, inflexible, scared.*

Again, there is no "right" way to becoming intimate with your feelings. What is most important is simply to practice talking to and looking into the heat of your experience, not away.

One thing I know for sure: we relive until we are set free. We relive until we are loved back to wholeness. We are not meant to hold on to fear and pain. In the beginning, we are free in love, and in the end, we will return to that love. The in-between, however, is of our choosing.

Once again, I remind you that it is in turning toward the knot, the fire, the bleeding that we begin to empty ourselves of lingering soreness.

I know I am being invited to heal something hurting within me when I find myself trying to escape through a daydream. If things have been especially challenging with my two little ones, for instance, when I have been quick to anger, I often fall into a deep rut of shame around my unloving behavior. Then, instead of tending to my shame with love, I escape into the unhealthy habit of wishing or dreaming for something different.

I will start fantasizing about a life without children, which then morphs into a painful regret of having children, and then, before you know it, I'm neck deep in an awful place of wishing for a different, better life where none of this agony exists. I do all of this to avoid admitting to painful actions and feelings. I create an entirely alternate universe with the hope of evading my own heart and soreness, and this only creates more pain and distress.

The very moment I inflict hurt and swirl into angry contempt, life hands me an invitation, which I ignore by neglecting my body's cries to regain harmony. The pain then deepens and lodges. My body replies with all sorts of uncomfortable feelings to signal my disconnect from the heart, and I am dragged down into the shadow world of myself, where I sit in the dark until I remember to speak each feeling brewing within me.

If I accept the summons of spirit and healing by going to a quiet room to sit down, slow my body and breath, place my hands over my heart, and let the feelings trapped inside me come and be named, I recover and heal.

I remember the last time this happened. I noticed I was beginning to drift into regret and resentment, so I went to a quiet room and faced my hurt.

I named:

Shame (pause and bow).

Fear (pause and bow).

Regret (pause and bow).

Anger, rage, embarrassment, stupidity, inability
to love, hopelessness, lack, hatred . . .

One after another, words, feelings, and stories spilled from me, each pulled from the storm and carefully placed like a flapping fish on the shore of awareness, no longer lost in the squall of shadow-land. I drew the names of each frantic voice from my unconscious depth and let each one be loved. I wept with each recognition. I cried because it took an incredible amount of vulnerability to admit what I desperately wanted to hide from, and even more vulnerability to love myself as I fumbled to honor my bravery and somehow cradle my mess.

After a few moments of raw and tender attention, a peaceful hush washed over and through me, as if a restless bunch of caged birds had been set free from my chest. And in that new space, I planted seeds of love and intention by praying a small prayer of gratitude to my higher self:

> Thank you for helping me to be here in this place of challenge and growth. For helping me to stay with myself in this moment, as I learn to heal what has become separate from my heart. Let me use these experiences of heartache and shame to bring me back to my nature of love and kindness. Thank you for helping me reverse the damage that has been done, with unwavering presence and compassion toward those I love, including myself. Thank you for helping me choose to heal, instead of escape. For helping me stay with myself, my softness, in this open state of receptivity and grace.

There is simply no living without this storm cycle. It is our deepest work to smooth the surface of our inner torments. It is our deepest work to begin loving all of ourselves, even that which we avoid, that which feels ugly and appalling. These places need us to allow them to speak and pass through so they don't harden over the light in our eyes and lodge in the corners of our jaw.

Instead of growing thick and dense with wildfire, we must learn to give name to each plume of smoke clouding our center. To pull all we feel, on a continual basis, into the soft spotlight of our attention. Let compassion meet flame. What is hot will cool. What is hard will grow soft once it is brought into the bright field of light and acceptance. What is stopping you from loving will bring you closer to love than anything else.

Struggle and suffering are always present. I have yet to meet a day where one or the other is not offered to me, and I know this is true for most of us. There may come a time when we will no longer accept their bidding, but until then, we must choose to ride these waves, respect our dark moments, and celebrate our victories in choosing more love. We must vow to stay with ourselves in all ways. We must deny nothing its arrival.

In the act of gently turning ourselves over to our days and moments of grief, we accept their plea of healing and we in turn are taught a form of fearlessness. And from this fearlessness, we are given access to yet more love.

In this practice of awareness and turning toward our discomfort, all pain goes back to where it came from, and often leaves no trace of having been here, except for leaving us with a bit more space around our hearts, a little more spaciousness in our capacity to love, to give, to be with our lives. Time and again, pain comes, burrows deep, and then departs, clearing a space that benevolence and love always show up to fill, so long as we invite them through our loving awareness.

If we are wise, our suffering can be used as a powerful, peaceful call to opening and acceptance, for on the other side of travail is a surplus of love. Hardship does not come to pull us into despair, it comes to inspire growth and acceptance in all directions, across all time and space. It teaches us to hold moments and ourselves in a place of nonresistance and in so doing, shows us how to uncover our magnificent, fearless hearts.

If we do not run but rather comfort the uncomfortable, we dissolve our tense and frightful tendencies and incorporate ease into all of our encounters. These thorny moments are best not feared or avoided or even wished away; they are instructors on how to come into peaceful, intrepid oneness with every facet of our existence.

If you cannot transform your moments of discomfort, you will forever be running from your life. But if you learn to stay, you learn how to *be*.

In being, without avoidance, we learn that life, joy, abundance, strength, and healing are each born from the very earth we are standing on—never somewhere else, but in every moment, at all times, wherever we are. No pattern of detachment or avoidance from pain can ever work, for we carry it along with us until we decide to set it free.

♥

PRACTICE   Free the Feeling

(Listen to this audio meditation at sarahblondin.com/heart-minded-meditations)

Close your eyes. Inhale deeply, fill your lungs to capacity, and then slowly let your breath leave from your mouth. I want you to breathe deep into all the tight corners of your being.

We are not meant to hold on to anything we are not made of. This means your fears, your stress, your beliefs, and your endless list of burdens. Ever so graciously, your body is trying to instruct you to free the feelings keeping you bound. Nothing you feel is in vain or without meaning; each difficult feeling is a bubble of suffering trying to burst.

Imagine your body as the sea. Picture yourself as the great, wide ocean, with creatures of unique beauty playfully swimming in your water and ruby-colored coral in your sand. You are alive. You are tranquil. You are filled with awe.

Now imagine a bubble escaping up through the sand, and inside that bubble is a feeling that does not serve you. It is rising into your awareness. Do not try and push the bubble down. See it for what it is: something you are not made of trying to escape from within you.

Give a name to the bubble, a name of something you wish to let go of. It could be heartache or loneliness or something more specific, like a memory still rattling around inside you that you are tired of carrying.

Watch the bubble travel up to the surface of your water, sending it on its way with a sigh of gratitude and a warm smile, not annoyed by its presence, but purified.

Hardship is not punishment, dear one. Feelings are not punitive; they are bubbles of grace rising to the surface. Make friends with the shifting sands deep within you; you are opening, changing. Let the air that needs to be released release when and how it comes. Love these bubbles of grace. Curl the corners of your mouth into a small smile as they leave.

You may stay here watching and naming as many bubbles as you wish . . .

Open your eyes only once the water within you feels lighter. Once there has been a release inside of you. You don't need to pick back up any of these feelings, memories, or stories. You may leave them to rest now. You may be full of space. You are allowed to be, to breathe, and to live without them.

Belly soft, edges smooth. Be in peace, dear one.

8

RETRIEVAL OF
PERSONAL PERMISSION

Finding no explanation for the often-painful realities you will face, you will look to the external for something or someone to blame for your feelings. This you will do in hope of diverting attention from feeling your pain and to help confirm your closing, constricting, and protecting.

What you may not realize is that this act will take from you a large sum of your power. This power will then be held hostage by the thing you have named as responsible for your distress.

It will only be restored once you realize it is *you* who senses the disharmony. And it is you and only you who wields the power to reverse the damage. You are wholly responsible for what you see, feel, and perceive. Your unrealized strength is in how you choose to respond.

While walking down the stony path of blame and projection, you will begin to feel invisible fingers of light pulling open the corners of your closed eyelids, gently asking you to come awake. At the same time, you will sense some restless rumbling near your center. It will speak not in words but in subtle vibrations. It is there to call your attention inward.

If you accept its invitation and begin to explore within, great beauty will rise from an inner well of divinity. Your gaze will be drawn toward your center, and you will gradually pull your power back inside yourself as you stop looking to the external for redemption.

This discovery will then propel you forward. It will bring you to the great understanding that you are the gatekeeper and curator of your life.

If you are ever in an angry, hateful place, keep careful watch for the invisible fingers and the tug pulling you open and in. These feelings are there to help awaken your *Power of Permission*. Following your call inward will reveal how to claim authority over your life, authority over your feeling heart, and authority as both the giver and taker of love and kindness.

If you are wise, with time you will come to meet the savior of life. That savior is you.

A LETTER FROM THE UNIVERSE

As we open to the pervasive grace around and within us, allow our great feeling intelligence to guide us, and help our storms of hurt and residual pain move through us, we come awake. We recognize places we hadn't dared to look. We come to realize our power and understand that we are the gatekeepers and curators of our life. It becomes safer in self and body, for we are no longer hiding things away. Now it's time to weed our overgrown inner garden.

This garden comes with great responsibility. You cannot leave even the smallest weed unnoticed or unplucked from the soil, for if ignored, it will take root and grow into something far more challenging to remove later on.

We all want to reap the harvest, but few of us want to undertake the painstaking process of clearing the earth. The same is so for every human life. We long only for goodness, for calm seas, and an endless rotation of plum and pink dusks. When a weed grows deep and begins to choke our crops, we lament, point fingers, and avoid our duty. Something is operating within us that does not want to be awake and aware. I think of this as the force field of our ancestral lineage; it is the thick fog of our ancestral past. The heavy weight of our forefathers and mothers, who never fully learned about their own potency and power to choose their hearts.

If we are not conscious of this invisible force field, we will continue down the stony path of blame and projection and remain adrift in the sea of those lost from source and our birthright of joy.

My dad was born in 1948. He says his generation was taught to not speak of their feelings, let alone express or try and process them. He grew up hearing the famously destructive expression, "Children are meant to be seen, not heard." People had no words, no language to address the heart. Trauma it unnoticed, unhealed, and ignored, meaning that people were left alone with the confusing world churning around and within them. In essence, they were not allowed to convey their humanness.

If you slipped and expressed what was inside you, your pain would only increase, as you were often punished, shamed, ridiculed, or ignored for your "undignified" display. Unaware of an alternative way of being, people carried on with strained hearts and dimly lit spirits.

Many of us are from such lineages, where people simply steeped in silence and internalized their pain. The part of us that does not want to come back to life is the part still clinging to that very long line of constricted humans. When we choose to follow the call to come awake, we have to purposefully pull in the opposite direction of this force field, and that can seem like a very difficult thing to do. It takes ongoing effort to walk in the direction of our hearts and highest truth. In fact, for many of us this is the work of a lifetime, and yet it is also work that rewards us quickly and gives our life meaning, showing us that it is worth our effort. This hope only intensifies as we permit ourselves to come into alignment with our heart.

As we give ourselves permission to be led by our heart, we move into our highest human power. We wield a new strength. And with practice, we begin to see glimpses of our freedom.

In the times we choose to let go of angry voices and oppressing behaviors, our heart releases. We can feel it. Every molecule of our being rejoices. We become, for a small crack in time, eternal. This is what it feels like to be heart minded.

While our ancestors may not have known how to permit themselves to become heart minded, at your birth they whispered without words a message to your heart. They told you of their longing to see you grow and love like they could not. And they task us to do the same for our children. If we take on this sacred responsibility—not just for ourselves, but for our children—each new crop of souls has a chance to evolve beyond the last crop, to move a little closer to the lighthouse of their hearts.

It is easy to miss or resist this responsibility. It is easy to be comfortably uncomfortable living under the reign of this lineage of disconnection and dissonance. It is as if we would prefer to continue to be swept along rather than rise to our true power. We often feel the same about hard conversations or being held accountable by a friend. These calls encourage us to grow and expand, and yet often a part of us tries to writhe away or drag our feet. A part of us wants to stay asleep. We don't want to be held fully responsible for our actions or be liable for the ways we have caused harm.

But the truth always comes for us, even if we are walking in the opposite direction. This is why we eventually rise to the call to return to our wholeness, why the invisible fingers of light eventually succeed at pulling open our eyelids, why a roar eventually draws our attention inward.

♥

PRACTICE   I Give Myself Permission
(Listen to this audio meditation at sarahblondin.com/heart-minded-meditations)

Take heart. There is a part of you already wide-eyed and awake, one who can hear clearly, a far more powerful force of love and kindness beckoning you to move up and out of the unconscious fog. Now, let's allow this part to come out from hiding.

I'd like you to get comfortable and close your eyes. Feel your breath pulling you down and deep into your body. Feel that subtle and comforting feeling of home in yourself.

I know a part of you is afraid to come into your power. I know a part of you is afraid to hold your life with your own scared hands. I know a part of you is afraid, but I know another part of you is not. I know there is another part of you that is willing, starving for, and calling for all your gifts to be realized. I know a part of you is calling for your deeply caring self to rise. I know your heart speaks to you; I know you can hear it. I know you are working at listening … keep going, dear one. Keep rising above the fog.

This life is yours, sweet one. How would you like to live it?

If you long to move into the consciousness of your heart, say now:

I give myself total permission to become my heart.
I give myself total permission to become my heart.
I give myself total permission to become my heart.
I give myself total permission to become my heart.
I give myself total permission to become my heart.
I give myself total permission to become my heart.
I give myself total permission to become my heart.
I give myself total permission to become my heart.
I give myself total permission to become my heart.
I give myself total permission to become my heart.
I give myself total permission to become truth.

Say this, dear one, and know it to be true. Know that every part of your body, mind, and psyche believe you, that *you* believe you.

If inertia comes, if listlessness and despair grab at your ankles like weights pulling you away from the heart, if the fog slinks in through a crack, shake yourself awake again, dear one. Go back to this mantra as many times as you need, when you are most in need. Let it be your life raft. There is nothing more for you to act on, just repeat these words and let the grace of your summoned heart do the rest.

How beautiful you look, dear one. What light is pouring from you. From my heart to yours, I thank you for saying yes to how you most long to live.

Bow now to your own self in gratitude and open your eyes. All the light you see or feel around you in this moment is from your own spring. This is what it is to drink of your own nectar. This is what it is to be in your heart and true essence.

9

RETRIEVAL OF OUR
BODY OF LIGHT

Once fractured from origin and wholeness, you will feel as if you have been divided and split in two. At any given time, you will be operating under one or the other of these selves: the *Shadow of the Mind* or the *Body of Light*.

The Shadow of the Mind is governed by fear, constriction, and shadow. It is the part of you that has come to believe life is not safe, nor kind. It is the heavier, denser version of self, inflexible, blind to beauty, and rooted in its stories of woe and wound. It is constantly reliving the past and reaching for the future.

The Body of Light, by contrast, is governed by love, light, and kindness. It is the part of you still intact, connected to, and aligned with the divine source within you. It has complete trust in life, no matter its experience. It is your lightness. The without-walls, fluid, unstoried self, rich in beauty and rooted in devotion to the heart.

You will dip in and out of both realities. One will feel liberating, the other fraught with anxieties.

Coming to know the two aspects of yourself will temporarily cause pain and confusion. You will need to override your sense of powerlessness and learn how to navigate back to lightness if you're ever caught in the shadow. You will dance back and forth between the two, until you discover tools to dissolve and disengage from the Shadow of the Mind.

Do not forget: you are built of truth. Be wise when inhabiting the spell of darkness; it can and will serve as the portal into your lightness. It is your guide back to wholeness and it can teach you how to remove the divide between the two selves.

When you find yourself in the Shadow of the Mind, ask for the truth to be revealed. Give it love. Love is its weakness. If loved, it has little to stand on. Practice, diligently and earnestly, by giving more love, not less, to that which tries to steal your light. This is how you can restore your system to its natural state of equanimity and peace.

Remember this: you are made of truth. The rest is but an obscurity of your light.

A LETTER FROM THE UNIVERSE

We Should Talk About This Problem

There is a beautiful creature
Living in a hole you have dug.

So late at night
I set fruits and grains
And little pots of milk
Beside your soft earthen mounds,

and I often sing.

But still, my dear,
You do not come out.

I have fallen in love with Someone
Who hides inside you.

We should talk about this problem—
Otherwise, I will never leave you alone.

HAFIZ, *I HEARD GOD LAUGHING*

The moment we splintered from our hearts, while smooth-skinned babes, we were given—perhaps I will go so far as to say, gifted—a Shadow of the Mind. Its job is to protect the pure vulnerability of the heart. All these years it has been diligently working to protect what you unconsciously asked it to when you were struggling to make a safe place in this world, and it has helped you maneuver through life while feeling less susceptible to trauma. This shadow, however, sits like a stone in front of your entombed heart. It is time now to hold in your loving awareness this wounded protector, which has been blocking you from your light, for if you do not, you risk never finding your way back to your heart.

In its role as protector, the Shadow of the Mind instills fear when adversity strikes or when we try to grow beyond what we are used to, even if we are stepping into something we have long dreamed of. To the Shadow of the Mind, expansion means risking harm and hurt. In its great valor, it tries to override our aspirations by berating and belittling us or by keeping us caught up in anxiety-producing thoughts. It does this in an attempt to keep us safe. It will try to stop us from evolving and changing. It will do whatever it can to prevent us from following through with our deepest calls and dreams.

When we are not aware of the shadow's ways, we can become its captive and find it hard to move freely in our lives. Kim, a student of mine, told me that when lying on the floor for meditation, she would often feel overwhelmingly vulnerable. Being undefended, open, and receptive was so difficult. She recognized all the ways her body was contracting in "an effort at self-defense."

The revelation both startled and humbled her. Before this moment, she hadn't seen how her shadow was holding dominance over her body, but once aware, she was able to release it. This brought her to tears. Kim, like so many of us, was operating under the force of this shadow, and did not even realize its grip. We do not realize we are in an almost constant state of bracing ourselves, rather than opening up to our life.

When something in our life falls, ruptures, or shifts; when challenge or change sprawls forward; when a condition isn't met; or our perceived safety and comforts are threatened, the Shadow of the Mind rises up and assumes dominance. It rises up when grief knocks on our door. When we sit down to meditate and breathe and feel fear coming to the surface as we begin to meet ourselves. When life says that the ground you are standing on is not as solid as you thought. When a lover leaves, or a trust is betrayed; when an angry or harsh word guts us. Even when a love is realized, when dreams manifest, the Shadow of the Mind shows up to maintain safety and order. It tries to divert us from touching down in these places. It is what we hide behind most days and what stops us from living an emboldened life.

But here's the thing: you have the ultimate say. You get to say *no*, I am *ready* to face all the risks in order to live a more fully embodied and alive life.

It's worth pausing here to recognize that you have always held this power. The Body of Light has been there all along. But you need to relieve the shadow of its duty before you can give the wheel to your Body of Light and let it steer the ship.

I remember a time when my shadow engulfed me. I had just gotten a criticism of my writing and could feel the life draining from my body. My breath became rapid and short; my whole chest cavity felt like it was collapsing. To have something as precious and dear to me as my writing being torn apart was like suffering a stab to my very heart. I felt a deep inadequacy open inside me and I wanted to run from all the big feelings and voices pillorying me. You know those moments when it feels like too much? Too much to hold, too much to face, too much to stand in? This was one of those moments.

I went to my bathroom closet and found my little orange bottle of Valium. I had gotten a prescription to ease my fear of flying, but in this moment of crisis I wanted only to escape this storm and this overwhelming feeling of failure, and I knew this could offer me that. As I held one small blue pill in the palm of my hand, a voice spoke from deep inside me: *Escaping from pain ensures the return of this pain. Put the pill down and go outside.* I reluctantly put the pill back in the bottle and dragged myself out the door into the night air.

I began walking through the half snow–, half mud–covered meadow, the moon casting a cool blue light over everything. Thoughts of harsh self-criticism continued to gather momentum as I walked. It was as if my thoughts knew I was listening now and began their chorus of heart-wrenching debasement: *You can't do this*, the shadow howled. *Nothing you do will ever be good. Give up now.* With each cruel whip from my shadow's tongue I cried, and then all of the sudden I began to sing.

"Help. Please help me. Remind me why I am here. Remind me why I am here." With a shaking voice, I sang those words over and over to the wide-open field and sky.

My singing turned to sobbing; tears began pouring out of me. I kept walking until I couldn't. I kneeled at the roots of a dying maple tree, and as I wept, the most soft and loving presence began gently speaking. *You are all right*, it said. *You are all right.* It was so genuinely loving that I almost believed it.

I tried talking back. I said I didn't feel all right. I said I wanted to get away from this feeling. I was defeated, exhausted, and cold. I kept crying until I felt a bit lighter, and then I walked back inside.

My son was standing at the door and, looking into my heavy eyes, asked me if I wanted to dance. We turned the music up so loud it filled our whole house, and we moved. I moved. I let the drums and rhythm shake some of my pain loose. I danced until I felt warm again, until my blood was moving through me quickly.

And then . . . the quiet came. Stillness came. I ate dinner with my family, and afterward went to clear the table. With my arms full of dirty dishes, grace cracked open inside me and sent its gift of release and relief flooding through me.

I suddenly felt like I was okay. That everything was okay.

My grief had left me. I began to smile, and my eyes welled with tears. Not tears of sorrow, but of gratitude, tears of wonder, tears of joy. I looked at my husband and said, "Oh, my goodness, it's grace." He held me in a warm embrace and I silently said thank you to grace. I said thank you to myself for listening to my sorrow. I said thank you for the wisdom that led me to sing, to dance, to let go. I refused to run or remain immobile—I sang; I danced; I howled. I listened to the wild current of my feelings' needs. It was not beautiful, it was frightening—but in the end, I was free.

Had I taken the pill and escaped, I would have lost this invaluable moment. I would have lost the profound insight that our bodies know how to help us move through hard moments. They will support us if we are willing to be fearless in the face of our fear.

Grappling with my neurosis, I found my inner guidance system. I found my heart. I found even pleasure, for I was learning. I was collecting evidence on what I was capable of facing and transforming. I even came out of this struggle feeling less attached to and protective of my writing, more willing to learn, and less egotistical. I was discovering I wasn't alone, that even in my darkest night something within me was whispering me back to my own light. This something doesn't relieve us of feeling our upsets and discomfort but shows us a way through them.

My shadow was trying to protect me from feeling pain by trying to convince me that I needed to escape the narrow place, the part of me that felt so diminished by the criticism of my writing. It tried to keep me away from going toward it, but instead, the voice of my heart spoke and guided me through my upset and into a place of grace and acceptance.

I know my Shadow of the Mind intimately. I know it doesn't want me to grow, not because it is unkind, but because it is afraid. But the heart, the heart is not afraid, and if you are listening closely it will always show you how to let go and open to every moment of your life.

If you find yourself paralyzed in fear or anxiety, you can choose to turn toward the feelings gripping you instead of running from your shadow. You can even speak to this shadow, asking that it leave.

Once the Shadow of the Mind retreats, all actions, emotions, and responses can flow out of you at last. You will find yourself able to speak and move in ways that will help your body release the built-up tension and fear. The intelligence of your heart will show you how.

This takes practice. There's no such thing as an instant cure or permanent freedom from the shadow's grasp, but by accepting the duty to diligently tend and instruct this shadowy protector, you can come to realize that each time you are pulled toward your fear, you also have the chance to say no. You can strengthen the voice that pulls you away from fear and toward your highest good. You have the choice to slowly lift the veil from your heart and let it stretch out and fill you.

At the beginning of this chapter I said that we are "gifted" this shadow. Why did I say that? Here's how I see it: We are here to learn mastery of our own beings, to discover the divine and the many gifts within us. Until we learn for ourselves what we are capable of, we do not know. We cannot know our magnitude without pushing against the boundary of our distrust and doubt (the shadow). What better way to learn and discover our prodigiousness than through confrontation with its opposite?

In wrestling the shadow free, we awaken the dormant seed of our magnificent potential.

In *The Prophet*, poet Kahlil Gibran wrote: "Your joy is your sorrow unmasked," alluding to the fact that one must confront the shadow of sorrow or agony in order to find rapture for their life and their being. Just as the seed must push its way up through the dense matter of the earth, we too must push up and through the opaque mask of our shadow.

This is not to say we need an endless supply of pain and suffering in order to come out the other side, but that even after the inevitable mess of having turned from and armored our hearts, there is still alive and well within us a divine brilliance that is ours alone to discover and claim.

No victory is sweeter than connecting with our own hearts after chipping free the stone of our shadow. We find our true power through this confrontation, through our commitment, devotion, and reverence for the light of our true being.

PRACTICE   From Shadow to Light
(Listen to this audio meditation at sarahblondin.com/heart-minded-meditations)

To understand both shadow and light is to understand our essential duality, the internal battle being lived within each of us at our core. It is our responsibility to face our shadow so the light can pour in.

When you enter the territory of the Shadow of the Mind — you feel it. When you enter the relief of your Body of Light — you feel it. When you are in the trance of the shadow, all thoughts, emotions, and feelings feel dense and heavy. You are unwilling to soften or become tender. Things feel impossible, hostile, limited.

When in the shadow, you are ruled by scarcity and lack. Feeling any of these things is an indicator that you are wading in the waters of the shadow.

Please close your eyes and rest now, deepening and lengthening your breath. I'd like you to awaken a feeling of curiosity and wonderment at the possibility that you are the answer and antidote for everything you face in life.

There is a light in the very center of your being. Because of how life unfolds, you covered this light, dear one. You were trying to keep your sweet goodness safe from harm.

But when you covered this light, you entered the dark. You entered lack. You began to forget this light was even here. But it is still warm, still fervently burning in the core of you. The truth of who you are still lives.

Look into the eyes of the darkness and ask for your light to come forward. It is time; you are ready to reclaim your Body of Light. It's up to you to make it clear to your shadow that you, not it, are the authority over your body now.

I'd like for you to go within yourself and begin to look for your shadow's sticky fingers clinging to the edges of your heart. Then, begin a conversation.

Look inside for the loneliest, most sorrowful, indignant part of you. This is your frightened shadow. The aspect of you that is unwilling to open to love and expansion.

I'd like you to speak to it lovingly, yet firmly, asking it to leave your being now. Thank it for its efforts and assure it that you are okay and ready to take over, ready to trust in yourself and direct your life. Tell it that you are in charge now and it is time for it to rest.

You will not live one more day under the Shadow of the Mind's tyranny.

You are taking conscious and loving ownership, dear one, of your very being. Not only are you capable of doing this, you are longing for it. You are longing to assume this role. Let nothing lure you away from your mastery. If not now, when?

Now of course, life is going to resume its natural order, and the shadow will still come stinging through you at times and shock you into forgetting the pact you made. But so long as you can bring tender attention to it and be clear about who's in charge, you will keep moving toward heart mindedness; you will be supported and held by your heart, even in your most challenging times.

Remember, dear one, your shadow is not an enemy, not something to abuse and abolish. It can be used as a tool to help strengthen your resolve, so that you may keep learning to stretch into the gentle part of you that is motivated by love.

Open your eyes now and take joy from having experienced these moments of mastery of your own home and heart.

10

RETRIEVAL OF SHAMELESS VULNERABILITY

In order to step out from the protection of the Shadow of the Mind, we must no longer see our vulnerabilities as weakness. In truth, vulnerability is powerful wisdom. It is the quiet wisdom of our deepest, most truthful self. It can shift entire groups of people caught in war or in a battle of wills.

Gandhi, Mother Teresa, Jesus, Martin Luther King Jr., and Buddha were all vulnerable, compassionate, exuberant leaders who radiated love and kindness. Each one, in their own way, freed themselves of the shame associated with being sensitive and instead led with sensitivity as their greatest tool. They knew that they were being called to change the world and would have to persuade others to rise in goodness and not in fear. They knew that the only way to do this was by standing firmly in altruism and benevolence, in the soft earth at their core.

You can do the same.

From the moment you first wake in the morning, you can invoke the power of your feeling body by consciously setting the intention to allow yourself to be led by your unfettered heart. You can ask that your mind let down its guard and defenses.

With no protection placed on top of your softness, you will grow wild and unencumbered.

Make no mistake, being in the world without defense is not the easiest of places to be. We are used to being guarded and closed in order to prevent ourselves from being hurt and your sensitivity, when first exposed, might feel overwhelming and at times frightening. Initially, you may find yourself feeling embarrassed; people may criticize you. You may be objectified and scrutinized. This is only because people who don't yet know this way of being, who are themselves at a loss for how to approach their heart, will be both curious and frightened, which can lead them to lash out. Consider that they might be afraid of kindness, love, and vulnerability.

Meeting a very open spirit can bring up feelings of both magnetism and contempt, but while the people you encounter may at first feel those things, eventually some of them will also come to meet the love and openness in themselves. That's just the natural law. We are built open, but we learned to forget it. Fortunately for you and for all of us, it is also natural law that, if given time and opportunity, we will tend to edge ourselves back toward the light.

This remembering and forgetting our true nature doesn't just happen once in a lifetime, of course. Any time you feel overwhelmed and notice that your mind is starting to pull you down into the mire, you can start reopening and remembering who you really are by realigning with intention, asking your heart to take the lead, and offering one bit of love in the face of your fear. So that you don't become defensive or close up when people judge your openness, ask yourself how you can drop the stories the mind creates to keep you from living in the open and then find ways to hold yourself energetically with love and compassion.

If you hurt, give but one small offering of love in place of pain. If it makes you want to close and turn away, give but one small offering of love in place of avoidance. If all the walls around you have fallen to rubble at your feet, give but one small offering of love in place of your despair.

And if love itself feels impossible to find, invite and hold your grief. And watch as warmth rushes in to fill the chasm in front of you, rushes in to soothe and smooth each surface you are willing to expose.

Each time you shift yourself toward loving, you invest in and empower your heart muscle. You invest in and empower your truest self. These gentle acts of self-care will imbue you with a new kind of luminosity and transform your being. As you pull the fractured parts of yourself back into alignment and wholeness and refuse the negative chatter of the mind, you bring yourself into heart-minded living.

There is really no need to remain in bondage with your suffering. You are wonderfully wise and capable, in nearly every moment, of turning toward the love at your center. Let yourself reveal your heart and set your world free.

PRACTICE   The Heart Without a Wall

(Listen to this audio meditation at sarahblondin.com/heart-minded-meditations)

Close your eyes now. Let your body settle into its breath. Remind yourself of your intention and what has brought you to this moment. Let your heart speak to you.

Now, bring forward a memory of a time when you were shamed for expressing an emotion or feeling, a time when you felt that your softness was under attack. Notice how you felt inside, how you knew there was something wrong with the way you were being treated. I want you to turn toward this memory and wrap your arms around this frightened and hurting self. Hold this self until it feels warm, whisper a few words of loving encouragement, and allow yourself to lean into your own comforting and healing embrace.

Learning to hold ourselves in our rawness and upset invites vulnerability in place of our shame. It removes the cast around the heart.

May I ask you, dear one, what is ailing you? What is lingering inside that you are denying? What are you neglecting to hold? Whatever is there, whatever sits in the dark belly of you, you need not hide. You need not fear; you need not starve or punish.

You have these hands, these arms, this heart, this breath, and this primal knowing that you are so deeply meant for loving. So, hold yourself, dear one. May you wake to your own inherent powers of comforting. May a memory wake in you the powers of your own abilities not to shy away from the wound, but to courageously rise to put pressure on what hurts and warmth on what stings. May you awaken your awe-some inherent powers to hold. May you become the mother you most need.

When the walls around the heart come down, you will feel surface pain and discomfort in cracking the veneer. Think of this discomfort as the same freeing pain of removing a cast from a once-broken bone. This temporary pain of cracking the cast off is an endurable, even joyful, pain. You can use your heart again! Smile, dear one, you are setting your precious self free.

Through the reawakening of our feeling selves and hearts, we not only learn to chew and digest the sour, but will taste the goodness, the sweetness, the nectar of life.

Circling back into wholeness will spark pathways of light that travel through the length of our bodies. It will spark a light so bright it radiates out and around us, with an aura that magnetizes us to all that is good and beautiful.

Your eyes will begin to recognize the magnificent in the mundane. The heart will speak louder than the critical mind. Your "needing to know" will be replaced with buoyancy and faith, a greater peace and acceptance for the unfolding.

With each thorn you remove, a beam of light is given. With each loving embrace you offer to that which snarls, a zephyr of certitude and trust in the unknown is revealed. You mustn't forget, as you endeavor to reach back to source and sensitivity, that in every challenge, something precious is given.

11

SOUL-ITUDE

Life will be abuzz around you, making it hard for you to maintain a connection with your inner compass and intuition. Without attention, your internal world often mirrors the noise level and distraction of your external one. The less time you spend nurturing the quiet waters within you, the more convoluted and muddled you will become.

If this goes on long enough, your interior reality will so distort that you will no longer be able to decipher your own feelings and thoughts. Many of your decisions will not be your own. You will need to find your way back to your own wealth.

To do this, you will have to challenge yourself by pulling away from the large and loud flurry of civilization in order to awaken your own feeling body and self. You will have to enter your own solitude.

This will be a challenge simply because it will seem as if you are swimming against the tide, moving in the opposite direction of the momentum around you. The initial suspension from doing and acting on autopilot will be the most painstaking part of the process. Know that the first moments will be the hardest, but once you crest above the noise, you will come to blissful silence. This is where you will meet your own wealth and guidance.

While you may have come to believe that stillness and quiet are lacking and void, you will come to learn that the very opposite is true.

You will arrive in the sunlit field of your own inner kingdom. This will take practice and a commitment to keep choosing to go within. Once removed from the raging river of doing and achieving, you will unearth your own unique voice and purpose.

Once back in line with your own system of guidance, you will begin to feel again. Light will spill over every surface of your life, for you will have discovered, in the quiet stillness, your true essence.

Wherever you are in life, be careful not to get swept into the current of noise. It will carry you to places not chosen by you. With each step you take, be sure to feel the earth underneath the soles of your feet and keep your focus fixed on your heart space; this will help to keep you grounded in the peaceful rhythm of true nature.

Truth will always be calling. Create space to listen, and you will hear it.

A LETTER FROM THE UNIVERSE

I asked for truth and was given silence.
I asked for truth and was stripped clean of my image.
I asked for truth and all that I believed had meaning
broke within me and outside of me.

I asked for truth.
I did not realize I was asking that I be emptied.

One of the most profound consequences of becoming closed off from our hearts is our inability to now *be* with ourselves. In our unwillingness to *feel*—to feel our pain, our feelings, our sensitivities—our bodies become the thing we leave instead of love. We spend most of our lives distracting ourselves and avoiding stillness because of this.

Time in solitude, or as I like to call it, *soul-itude,* is the only antidote. It can be one of the most challenging places to be. But in order for us to heal and embody our heart-minded selves, we must come to sit and listen in the quiet of ourselves. Without this, we cannot hear the wisdom of our hearts, we do not connect with "the still small voice inside," and we never come to realize our spiritual natures.

For you to begin healing and connecting with your most-wise center, it first helps to look at how you unwittingly avoid it.

Most of us spend our lives at the surface, working in endless circles. We loop around our relationships and our careers and our creative pursuits. We put most of our focus and attention on outcomes, and we devote our time to chasing them around until we are ready to move on to the next one. We then quickly attach to another, and busy ourselves with that chase—and the cycle continues. Because of our constant busyness, our ricocheting from one project to another, part of us is always thirsty, never slaked, forever looking to the next person or project to give us a feeling of meaning and worth. But there all along, in between doing and obsessing and dreaming and hoping and chasing, is where our relationship with our self and heart lives. It is where we find this abandoned part of us that we have made ourselves too busy to feel.

Where are you most living your life? This question came to me in a quiet moment in between my own doing. I sat, eyes closed, trying to calm and cool my overly active mind. For months I had been pouring myself, my thoughts, and my inspiration into this book. Very little else was allowed in. To stop and be still, to drink of the calm and peace on the outskirts of my creativity felt too hard, too ordinary, and too quiet. Yet when I arrived in a quiet moment, I saw that nothing held any meaning if I wasn't also in relationship with myself. If I could not tend lovingly to the quiet, I would spend a lifetime collecting things that would hold little if any worth in the end.

Reflecting on how we treat ourselves without the security blanket of our achievements will expose how we are treating the foundation of our life:

> Am I engaging with myself in loving
> ways through meditation or inquiry, so
> I can discover what I really need?

> Am I carving out time to be in solitude and simplicity?

> Am I spending my extra time lost in the
> distraction of my phone or computer screen?

> Am I busy trying to confirm my value
> and worth through others?

> Am I present with those I love when I am with them?

How much time am I spending giving myself
the love I endeavor to give to others?

What is the quality of my life when I am
alone in the moments between doing?

This life in between doing is where you meet your self. It is where you come to feel the comfort or discomfort of the relationship you have with *you*. It is in this space that you will feel the pain of dissonance from your heart. This is where we meet our shame, our self-loathing, our loneliness, our unaddressed pain, our numbing habits, and our tendency to disconnect and avoid our self. We avoid it because we have not fully learned to love our self and are at a loss for how to sit in solitude comfortably. It's a natural tendency to distract and avoid, which only compounds the disconnect and causes us to become more and more separate from ourselves.

But figuring out how to love who we are, as we are, alone in the present moment, is the work that will ultimately comfort and fill us. If you have a sincere longing to find peace and love in your life, you must first come to find both of these things *within* you. Instead of distracting and avoiding, it's time to kneel at your own feet and begin speaking softly to this core self you barely touch.

Because most, if not all, of us were reared to focus on outward gains—to earn love, achieve worth, and find purpose out in the world—when we consider pulling away and making a purposeful submersion into solitude, we threaten our own sense of importance. Choosing solitude challenges the very identity we have worked so hard to build. This, to many of us, is akin to a type of death. Pull away from our regular doing, striving, and achieving, and we face a sort of social suicide, or risk being forgotten. Or so we fear. This is why we remain so tethered to the external world and the identities we create to work "successfully" within it. It's as if our very lives depend on it.

We fear solitude, we fear sitting in our discomfort, we fear unplugging from our devices and engaging with the present moment and ourselves. We are afraid we will become irrelevant.

But in order to become heart minded and to discover who we are and what we feel, we need to slow down. We need to be willing to "fall behind" in order to fall within.

I know how scary or intimidating it can be to disconnect, to walk in the opposite direction of all that bright, shiny, noisy distraction. I have faced that fear again and again as I have answered my own call to stillness. But no matter the size of aversion or fear, you must trust me when I say that all that will matter, all that will ever amount to anything, is the relationship you have with the world you carry around inside of you. The heart speaks to those who become still in its presence. It cannot give you what you need unless you plant your feet, your whole being, before it.

In order to become heart minded, you must commit daily to coaxing forward your most tender and authentic version of self. You must commit to bridging the divide between mind and heart. It's nonnegotiable. You must have a daily practice or a regular period of time when you are in a state of solitude and non-doing.

You must enter the silence.

Trust that if you stay in the quiet and don't numb or distract yourself with stimulation, your heart, your essence, will reveal itself. Before this can happen, however, you will have to sift through the patterns and tendencies that have been stopping you from deepening this relationship with self. You will have to have your heart broken open.

I endured this process when pregnant with my first son and when my husband and I decided to move from the city to the countryside. While I was driven by some inner call to find solitude and stillness, I did not fully comprehend what would transpire as I moved from busying to quieting. While, to an outsider, it may have looked like a graceful transition into a world of tremendous natural beauty and space, I, in fact, encountered within myself quite an uncomfortable resistance to my new reality.

Having your heart broken open is not as beautiful as it sounds.

Indeed, having your heart broken open can, at first, be very much like being broken, like being shattered. Looking back, I see a woman who was struggling through a move to the country and struggling with being born as a mother. I see a shell of a woman. She looked sunken and tired, depleted and forlorn. She looked swollen in breast and hip. She was crawling on hands and knees from moment to moment, kept alive by only the breath she was given. The world had gone pale, through her eyes. She was disappearing. Journeying from one veil to another, a ghost of who she thought she was and unaware of what she was becoming.

With no easy places to escape to—like yoga studios, cafes, and friendships—I had to learn to stay in the quiet, when normally I would have run. I had to shed the layers of my distracted mind and its need for constant stimulation; I had to face my fear of silence, my fear of myself. My fear of the rawness of true presence.

I had to learn to observe my habits, my grasping for worth and meaning and my almost compulsive need to armor myself when feeling vulnerable and afraid. I had to see myself completely and come face-to-face with everything I had avoided exploring, admitting, and feeling.

I realized I had no idea how to be me. Me in the quiet, me in simplicity. Me without others. I had no idea who I really was. I spent nearly two years in deep introspection and purging. To quote Sue Monk Kidd from her book *When the Heart Waits: Spiritual Direction for Life's Sacred Questions*, it was "a passionate and contemplative crucible in which new life and spiritual wholeness can be birthed."

I dug in deeper than I ever had before and listened inside myself for guidance. I became skillful at listening to my intuition. I asked the open sky for help. I kneeled on the earth often. I made friends with the swallow, the raven, the owl. I cried without embarrassment. I called on my ancestors for help. I wrote every day. I admitted everything to the page. By speaking what was true for me moment by moment, I was strengthening my voice. I was pulling my fears and emotions out from the shadow of shame and avoidance and was in turn becoming whole. Nothing was left out of my loving awareness. I was caring for both the beauty and the strife of my life. I was caring for the ever-shifting current of my *truth*.

In time, my depression turned to joy. My fear to freedom. It was in solitude that I found, underneath all of the things I had spent my lifetime running from, a pearl of refined and humble beauty. I had reunited with the gift of my humanness, the undeniable grace and love that emanates from each of us at our core.

Discovering new land is terrifying at first. To be an explorer of the human experience means to be pulled through the many tastes, smells, and sounds of being alive. And if you are an explorer of the heart, you will be broken open and born vulnerable as a newborn babe, not once, but many times in your life. If you are there now—in that strange, dark land—I urge you not to resist. Look deeply for the part of yourself that is reaching out to catch you as you fall toward yourself.

There is no meeting the more expansive you—the heart-led you, your spirit—without a free fall into the unknown.

If you cannot feel ground—*good*.

If you cannot breathe without saying a
prayer with each breath—*good*.

If you cannot recognize yourself, and all
seems dark before you—*good*, dear one.

This is what the heart being broken open looks like. This is how we meet our deeper truth. First the heartbreak, then the reunion.

The more time you give to the internal realms, the more you will begin to detach from the thoughts, patterns, and beliefs that do not serve you: patterns and beliefs that block and barricade you from your heart. This is the gift of presence. When we sit and work at unmasking ourselves, we find that our spirit calls us forward to our own healing and helps us excavate our truest self and heart.

Immersion into myself brought me to both an insanity and a revelation I never could have imagined. It is how I know that if we wish to find truth, we must first meet the untrue. It is how I know that you should not be disheartened or frightened away if pain is what you first meet while visiting the quiet earth within you. The pain you may encounter is merely the cry of the most abandoned part of you, groaning with relief upon touchdown.

On the other side of jagged hurt is breath, wide-open sky, your intrinsic nature. Your unstoried, unburdened self.

I can promise you this. You will, with practice, persistence, and great attentive tenderness, be able to puncture the sting and come to where your place of healing resides. It is because of the discoveries I found in solitude that I devoted my life to clearing space for the spirit to speak, which allows us to become fluent in the language of the heart.

Of course, you do not need to move to the countryside, as I did, to engage with solitude (however, I highly recommend it if you are able). You can use the available time you have to engage quietly with yourself, to marinate in the sacredness of your being. Before I was able to learn from my heart, I was devoted to the tending of my inner world and becoming still. Before my work began helping and serving others, it was sincere and honest self-reflection and investigation.

Committing to time alone with myself transformed my life. What might shift in you if you found small ways to do this for yourself?

No two journeys into the self are the same. Solitude may elicit feelings of distress for some and feel like immense freedom to others. Inevitably, we will all stumble onto something painful. It is imperative that you learn to sit with your soreness and stagnant wounds. When you stop avoiding yourself—and begin deeply listening and following through with what glimpses and whispers of guidance come to you—you are led toward and then through your pain, while discovering self-acceptance, self-love, and compassion along the way.

If you feel afraid to sit with yourself and to meet and listen to your heart, ask yourself if this fear is worth the sorrow, disconnect, and static you sometimes feel lost in. Ask yourself if the price you are paying by listening to your fear is worth the sacrifice of living in alignment with your heart.

I'm reasonably certain—at least my hope for you is—that your answer will be a resounding no. No amount of fear can justify keeping yourself from fully experiencing this exquisite gift of life.

PRACTICE   Sitting and Staying

(Listen to this audio meditation at sarahblondin.com/heart-minded-meditations)

I'd like you to close your eyes now and bring all your attention to your breath, letting it gift you peace. Being quiet, picture raindrops falling onto your face, each drop of water bringing life to your earth — your body.

May I ask you, dear one, where are you most living your life?

I know you are afraid of the quiet you sometimes meet in the middle of your doing and at the end of the day. I know you feel like running away from it, but I want you to try and trust this quiet. When it comes, see it as an invitation to meet spirit, to meet heart, to meet yourself. This fear is but the deep soul ache of a self once lost, calling for a way home.

Do not fear yourself or anything inside of you. Trust the love and kindness of your being, knowing that on the other side of the discomfort is a pool of unconditional love. Reach deep into the densest part of your avoidance and wait, as the heart finds its way to you. Simply stay in the quiet one moment longer than you think you can … and then one moment more. Let your true self be remembered.

If a burden or fear comes up from the silence and makes you want to run, you must know that no amount of running will relieve you of these things, dear one. These seemingly impenetrable places are a part of you, and they live in you, like a fog that is waiting to be lifted. Before the fog can lift, however, it needs your attention. Part of healing is simply seeing the tangled vines and the foggy places within us. In practicing seeing, we activate spontaneous healing. If a stressful thought arises, watch as it comes and then leaves of its own accord. If you do not engage, it will leave on its own. See these thoughts, these places of strain, as habits: deep habitual thoughts that have long been telling the same story. They are not you; they are but the web of the mind woven on top of your true being.

If you feel lonely in this place, frightened of the unknown, or scared of what you may find, all you must do is begin speaking to these fears, this loneliness.

Make friends with all of yourself, by sitting with and being witness to every beautiful facet of your being. This life is for you, dear one; please do not spend it locked in your fear. Discover what you are capable of by learning to sit and listen to all of you. You are so very wise within. You are so very noble to begin to discover this for yourself.

I pray that you learn to stop, dear one, so that you may come fully into your body, your essence, and your light, so you may be fed. Be loved. Be accepted by you. And then see what comes of your discomfort. Often what comes of your pain is an opening into the very grace you keep thinking is evading you. This quiet universe you keep running from is the home of your most authentic, eternal source of self.

Now open your eyes, take a deep inhale and exhale, and say thank you to yourself, for being here, for caring, for endeavoring to love every inch of you.

Once you have learned to settle into the silence and solitude, you can begin summoning and listening for guidance and support. If it's love you want to build resonance with, the first step is intention and asking for it to come alive. Request this of yourself. Ask yourself, or the unseen forces that support you, for it to be revealed.

You may notice small voices and cries from some deep place within you, asking for seemingly random things: *Go outside. Move your body. Sit in silence. Find art supplies and create.* Heed these voices. They are helping you bring forth, through tiny requests, things that will bring your spirit more *alive*.

After becoming receptive, your only task will be to listen and follow through. The more you follow through with the guidance, the more you will be pulled into your center and well of wisdom and love. This process will gradually bring you closer and closer to the source within you. Love and kindness will breathe you back to life.

Do not be wary if your guidance has told you to leave a relationship or a job that is creating dissonance in you and feeding a dark part of you. You must listen. You don't need to act just yet, but you must listen. This listening and discovery may bring great waves of despair, loss, loneliness, fear, and grief, but you must hold. Hold to your intention; treat these deep requests with great reverence. Wait in patience, in tender openness, for the storm to clear and the wreckage to be released.

Coming into line with our source of love can mean, and often does mean, a confronting of each place where we are not in proper alignment—in places of love, work, and thoughts. In order to restore your body and self to unity, all the incongruences within you must be brought forth. Do not fear, even if the prospect is upheaval. Recall the practices held in these pages and know you are able.

As you begin following through with your requests, the voice of your intuition will get louder and wilder. It will sound less and less like a whisper and more and more like your own full voice. The more you respond to the call, the more you will feel love suffuse your body and the easier it will become to breathe, move, create, and, yes, give and receive love.

Honoring your body's calls is what heals your foundation and brings your feeling intelligence of love and kindness back into proper functioning.

When we listen closely, we are instructed to moments, things, words, and worlds that awaken a deep and profound sense of comfort and joy. May you be a student of your spirit. May you fill the small corners of the world with things you *love*. May you discover that it is *you* you must learn to love most and *you* who will show you how. It is *you* you are most longing to know, so hush . . . listen . . . follow through.

This is not risky. All stillness and listening leads to untapped resources of unending gifts tailored just for you. This is what liberation on the level of the soul looks like. It invites you to bring all of your gifts to life and to this world, and in doing so, lifts you up and out from the frenetic noise.

If rubbed, the leaves of purple sage will release their dynamic smell, but if left untouched they will keep their gifts hidden. Beneath the carapace of hard rocks live labyrinths of crystal. Within a tree, past its fortress of bark, lie rivers of water and sap. In the center of a flower is nectar fine enough to spin into honey. Deep within the center of all living things is a heartbeat and well of tremendous beauty. Valleys, rivers, pools of starlight. We marvel at life outside of us but never gaze within ourselves with the same amazement and worship. Never unearth our sweetness, our crystal, our deep rivers of water and sap.

An exploration waits within, an adventure of awakening, but we must be willing to go beyond the thick borders of our protective sheaths to find what is uniquely ours.

12

CULTIVATE LOVE OF THE SELF

*Love of the self is
the undoing of the woundings,
the undoing of our history,
our memories of hurt,
of all the things
that are keeping us away from love.*

Love of the self is to reach out and take our own hand.

Now that we have brought the neglected elements of ourselves and our experience into our loving ownership and awareness, we must learn how to love ourselves just as we are, as this feeling, fluid, learning, human self. We must learn how to cultivate and strengthen the muscle of love for our self. This is a very weak muscle for most of us, as we have been taught, inadvertently, to hate ourselves. The miraculous thing I've learned, though, through my experience with self-love and from feedback I've received from students, is that once you begin to practice it, your love starts to swell and saturate you with very little effort or time. It is as if there is a source waiting dormant under the surface of your awareness, that once focused on and summoned, erupts like a geyser to flood, imbue, and support you. This love is neutral and unattached. It is love in its purest form.

When we become radiant with our own love, we offer ourselves as medicine to the world. When we love ourselves, our eyes no longer write the story of hurt over the surface of our lives. Whether crooked stick or broken board, we begin to see life from a place of companionship, understanding, and compassion. To cultivate and find love for the self is to find love for our lives, and to find love for our lives is to find love for *all of life*.

The meditation and practice I share in this chapter has been listened to over a million times by people all over the world. Many of these listeners have shared with me stories of heart awakenings thanks to the simple practice of self-love. Some said they were brought to tears by it, and expressed having a "spiritual, life-changing rebirth" of themselves.

One woman said, "I could literally feel the shift within myself telling me that this is what I needed to feel whole again. To love myself and listen to my inner being because it will tell me what I need."

A startling number admitted how most of their lives were spent feeling estranged from themselves, and how their own tender loving has been what brought them the most healing. "My soul feels finally soothed after fifty-one years of struggle and misunderstanding, and I actually do feel I have come home," shared one woman.

It was hearing about shifts like these that led me to believe it is *imperative* that we learn to love the self *now*. We deserve to feel at home in our beings, in our bodies, in our hearts, and in our lives. We must start to teach ourselves and our children how to do this. There is love, just waiting like a sun within our chest, to affirm our value, our potential, and our light.

I was thirty-three years old when I said "I love you" to myself for the first time. And after, I wept from an unfamiliar place. It felt as if I was tying back to myself loose threads that had broken off years ago. I mourned the decades I had spent in disharmony with my body and being. In saying these three little words, however, I began to repair and mend this discourse. The love and acceptance I had been searching for in my life were mine already, awaiting their unearthing and rousing. I had everything I needed within me. I met for the first time—more alive and true than anything I'd ever known in my life—my own wealth, my sustainer. My birthright.

Because most of us are not taught self-love as young children, it's easy to splinter off from our inborn perfection, and before we know what's happening we enter the land of inadequacy. From this sense of being unlovable and "not enough," we then spend our days searching for ways to fill the giant hole in our souls.

To the people who come and go in our lives, we say, "love me;" we say, "give to me what is lacking;" we say, "bring me to greater love;" we say, "heal what aches;" we say, "fill what feels hollow." We say all of these things but never find the one person who can give us what we so desperately seek. And that is precisely because the love can't be found "out there." It's been "in here" all along.

After my revelation, I began saying "I love you" to myself, to my heart, every day. Try it. Begin your day by saying "I love you" to yourself. I'm willing to bet you, too, will find that with daily practice and time, you will begin to notice a shift. What once felt empty will begin to fill. What once felt desperate will start to feel hopeful. As we stitch together the divide we created within ourselves and step into our wholeness, lit from within by our own love and kindness, we heal and transform.

There is even data that confirms the value and importance of this kind of nurturance. In her book *Good Morning, I Love You*, psychology professor Shauna Shapiro cites research showing that the part of the brain responsible for growth and change actually shuts down when we are in shame and judgment and activates when we express self-compassion and love. Our bodies begin to flourish from our loving attention; *we* begin to flourish.

When I first began my practice of self-love, it felt like a bud beginning to open, petal by petal, within me. It was my body and heart, relaxing into openness from the love I was watering it with. The self-compassion and care I was learning to show myself was helping me feel and grow into the rapture of my own being. It was bringing me to the place where the love is deep within all of us.

Every day that we endeavor to love another, we must try to love ourselves first. Once we feel that self-love, all the other love flowing our way can uplift us to higher levels of love and joy. By no longer looking for love by giving love to others or trying to fill holes within ourselves, we are able to take in love as never before. And give it—without expectation—as never before.

If you ever find yourself consumed with troubling feelings of lack and unworthiness, pain or heartache, try to stop and get very still. Then, hold your heart and whisper, "I love you. I am listening."

I encourage you to speak lovingly to yourself daily, for this is how we disarm ourselves and invite our heart to come out of hiding. This is how we learn to free ourselves from painful relationships and heal scars within.

PRACTICE   The Breath of Love

(Listen to this audio meditation at sarahblondin.com/heart-minded-meditations)

Close your eyes now. If you are listening along, let the music fill your bones and dissolve your barriers. Let it lift the veil between worlds … let it soften you … breathe.

May I ask you, dear one, what do you see when you hold a mirror in front of you?

Do you look at yourself through eyes of love?

Of compassion?

Of kindness?

Do you look upon yourself as an evolving art piece?

Or do you see the lines of your furrowed brow?

Your shame hidden behind your eyes?

How, dear one, do you behold yourself?

Please place one hand on your heart and the other on your stomach. Lovingly hold yourself and repeat after me:

I love you; I am listening.

Are you able to feel a quality of presence come forward inside of you when you say this to yourself? The self that arrives when you touch your heart and speak lovingly to it? Are you able to recognize the unsullied self living inside of you?

This, my dear one, is your unstoried self. The gentle love that lives inside you. The gentle light. The self free from limits, from heavy identities. How beautiful you are, there behind your image.

Still holding your heart, head slightly bowed, repeat again after me:

I love you. I love you. I love you. I love you. I love you. I love you.
I love you.

You deserve nothing but love. Forgive whatever forces made you believe otherwise. Forgive the other hearts lost from their own love. Forgive the other hands that hurt and the other beings hurting. Remember the wellspring within you. Shake your love awake.

You are not lacking love, dear one. It is yours, here within you at all times. This is the breath of love running through you. There is a never-ending supply of it. Just be here and drink of your nature. You are love, you are love, you are love.

Breathe, holding yourself gently. Inhale and exhale, growing full on your own beauty with each inhale. Let all searching outside yourself stop here.

Take a moment to realize that your source of unending nourishment and love has been inside of you all along, within your own heart. Rest as this love.

When the world gets too big in ways that don't allow you to feel this part of you or when you have forgotten to tend to your own being, find a way to stop. Find your way back here. Only you can bring yourself here.

Let speaking to your heart take the lead as often as you can remember to do it, for in so doing, your sense of need and lack will diminish as you embody your own great beauty.

Learn how well you can nourish yourself using your own hands, your own voice, your own heart. You see, once we are in touch with our inexhaustible supply of self-love, we can give without condition, we can walk without weight, and we can heal whatever it is we temporarily forgot in our humanness.

And if, dear one, you are having trouble feeling this love instantly or at all, I promise you, if you are earnest, if you are sincere and disciplined, in time some small world of light will crack open inside of you and lead you back to your heart. Just keep offering yourself love, and you will begin to believe.

Nothing is outside of you. Your own kingdom of fulfillment is within.

PART 2

DEEP TISSUE MASSAGE
OF THE SPIRIT

A small seed felt the sun of my caring shining upon it and began
to spread up through the black earth. I found in the dark, there
was life, just waiting, ever so patiently, to be fed by my attention
and loving devotion. My pain was the usher of new life.

The goal of part 2 is to support you through the rough
spots of your journey. These practices are meant to
be your life raft when traversing through the dark.
Remember, there is no shame in encountering what
is hard and uncomfortable; all pain can be your portal
to the divine. If not approached with fear, these places
can help to reveal hidden gifts and strengths and can
assist you in excavating a self you love and believe in.

13

THE SLEEPY UNDERTOW

An expanded version of yourself is being birthed alongside the painful dissolving of the other. Be gentle. Befriend faith and fortitude. This is a slow process. Not easy, but necessary.

You are a pilgrim of spiritual awareness. You are stepping toward wholeness. Therefore, you must face the great opposing forces. Your liberation will require true grit. Remember, you know how to hold yourself. You can soothe your own body and mind as you travel through the debris.

Know that no matter how far from complete something feels, it is always the opposite. Most people give up just as they are about to receive the gifts of their efforts. Keep hand on heart, stay quiet in mind, and breathe slow and long.

Fiber by fiber, one molecule at a time, you are coming home.

A LETTER FROM THE UNIVERSE

Reuniting with your heart and truth is not linear. It is more like moving through peaks and valleys, winter and spring, calm and storm. It is picking up the pieces after the wreckage and learning how to build a more beautiful, more authentic vessel, again and again.

The new awakenings and understandings revealed in this book and in you will become a mountain of truth. You are coming to know how to realign with your heart and self, and now you must learn to scale the mountain of your truth, dear one. This is a powerful stage in your journey toward wholeness, but before you are fully able to explore the landscape of your truest version of self, you must become aware of what will come to meet you in opposition as you try to move ahead.

A common thing I hear my students struggle with is how to stay awake and in the heart. They find that they touch into the truth of their most expanded and enlightened self, and soon after fall back into the well-rutted roads of their old and tired behaviors. They open briefly and then snap closed again, seemingly against their will and out of their control.

Why does this happen?

As I understand it, with any powerful surge forward there is an equally powerful counter to this momentum. You are advancing through something, which means you, at the same time, are moving against something else. This something I call *The Sleepy Undertow*. It's a very mighty force that, like the ocean's undertow, will drag you back out to sea just when you've raised your head above water to breathe.

In this practice, this can look like taking great strides into heart-inspired living and being, and soon after, dramatically returning to old patterns, sabotaging healthy choices you made, and re-armoring yourself with negative beliefs and thoughts.

I noticed this force each time I came to understand something that was bringing me closer to my freedom. The more heart centered I became, the louder an opposing voice or energy became, as if to try and take from me my newfound openness. It spoke in a berating tone that would belittle my discovery, telling me I wasn't becoming more expansive, but rather, deluding myself.

For a long time, I took this voice to be my own and would let it drag me back down into my despair and hopelessness. Then I realized this was where I was going wrong. I began to sense this voice or energy as the opposing force to our light. As you gain momentum and understanding, it begins to clap and boom like thunder and lightning, creating a storm to try and distance you from beauty and seeing. Why? Because that is its job. I saw, in a moment of clarity, that it had nothing personally invested in me, and I understood it was but the job of "the other." It was not personal, yet I was making it so. When it surfaced, I identified with it and in so doing fell back into the sleepy abyss I was trying so hard to rise out of.

If you too have sensed a lurking shadow of despair in your most expansive states, perhaps you have met with The Sleepy Undertow. If you feel its presence, calmly address it with love and breathe it free from you, for this force is not you. It is an impersonal aspect of the unconscious playing its role in our journey toward freedom.

You are the light. You are the pearl being made in the mouth of a shell at the bottom of the sea.

14

COMFORT WHEN NUMB

The Sleepy Undertow also disguises itself in apathy—or numbness. It is a common symptom of being disconnected from our hearts and our feeling bodies. It is the sense that even with all we are grateful for, we cannot appreciate, taste, or feel our blessings. The sun shines, but we are not warmed. The day begins and ends, and nowhere during our waking hours were we able to connect with sincerity to anything.

This numbing happens when we are lost in a story of suffering and have become snagged by a belief or identity that has dragged us to the dark side. It is how our unconscious feelings and thoughts can sometimes grab hold of us and pull us away from our heart center and into sleep.

If we start believing that our life doesn't measure up to a certain standard, or our image is threatened by something we've done or said, we can fall into a numb place where we're disconnected from heart and source. To get back into the heart and the flow of goodness, we must hold ourselves in this state of non-feeling with great gentleness.

I sometimes fall into a state of numbness or apathy after I've had a particularly challenging stint with my two little ones. I'll slowly slip into a familiar victim story of not having time for myself and how they take everything out of me. Usually, before I am even aware of what's happening, I find myself full of condemnation and hopelessness, and I numb out instead of facing the thoughts and feelings attached to this belief.

With practice, I have become much more skilled at catching the inner dialogue before it takes over, and even when I don't catch it early enough, I have gotten better at creating space so my feeling self and heart can come back to the surface.

For example, my three-year-old son recently had an epically rebellious week and I was becoming exhausted. I had little or no energy to put into my writing, which has always been my lifeline to my higher self and understanding, so I started feeling more and more compromised and began drifting into a state of hopeless and despairing thoughts.

Sensing the deadening numbness creeping over me, I asked my husband to watch our two sons so I could go for a walk alone in the nearby, snow-covered forest. I sat down on a fallen birch tree and tried to look for feeling within myself but was met with a throbbing, empty, blank space. I felt entirely numb. But slowly, right there in the space I had created around my passivity, another voice began to ask small things from me.

Follow the moose prints through the snow, the voice urged.

So, I listened. I followed. My attention was drawn out and away from me and into the natural simplicity of this present moment in nature.

The tracks led me to a creek bed, where the voice spoke again: *Now, sit here for a while and listen.* Again, I did as asked. Still numb, but now more focused on beauty and what was real in the moment, I got up and walked a bit farther. The voice kept repeating, *Let of the earth, lie on the earth. Let of the earth, lie on the earth.*

It took me awhile to realize that those were my next instructions.

I kneeled on the cold snow and lay down. I followed the voice and was next drawn onto my back, arms spread wide beside me. The sky was expansive, shifting, empty, fluid. There in my surrender, watching the dance between white wisp and blue, a crack opened within me—my feeling heart. I could feel myself swell out from the small confusion of my mind and I stretched with gratitude for the wisdom of my own self, the voice of my sweet heart, giving all it could to bring me home.

I was able to see my children not as burdens, but as gifts who were teaching me how to love myself and others. When I got home, I held them close and was able to continue on with the day, grounded in presence, patience, and acceptance, but most importantly, an open and willing heart.

You see, even in our numbness, something is speaking. A small voice within offers help and relief from our captivity. If, instead of running further from the place you are in, you can create space to be guided and instructed, you will be.

Unfortunately, in our discomfort and pain, we tend to busy instead of ground. We fill instead of hollow out. We create noise and distraction that does not allow us to hear what it is that we need. This is why we stay in places of disharmony longer than necessary.

If you have trouble hearing the voice of your sweet heart, just try for a moment to surrender to your suffering and create the space to listen. Perhaps you will be brought to your knees, heart exposed, against the earth. Surrender is often all that is needed for love and joy to come back into focus.

Your strength is in how you choose to mold your moments, your struggles, your pains, and the hard truths that confront you. It is not so important why or what has happened, but rather what you do when you come to your edge. Do you succumb and crumble, or do you respond and rise? If you focus on learning from these moments by bringing whatever besieges you into the light of your consciousness, that will be all the effort you need to make room within you to feel, truly feel, the blessings of your life without blocks or burdens. I know this to be true, not just for me, but for the hundreds of thousands of people I hear from who listen to my work.

With kind attention to what you encounter, you create an openness inside yourself that will set you free.

The voice of your sweet heart does not sound any different from your "regular" voice. It does not boom or speak with a different sound; it is you, speaking to you. Usually people can hear the heart voice around the borders of their wrought and stressful thoughts. You can tell what it is because it comes in to offer some support, whether it's *Take a bath* or *Put on some Mozart* or simply *Breathe*.

If you stop and listen beyond what you are worried about, you'll hear it—a quiet and gently encouraging cheerleader.

We often dismiss this voice and don't make space for it to be heard. Instead, we recycle the same thoughts, causing ourselves more distress, and end up getting lost in the mess. All you need to do, dear one, is slow down enough to hear it.

Numbness can also be seen as hopelessness. For one to find hope again, for one to feel alive again, one must find a vein to their heart. Instead of saying "I feel numb," say, "I want to feel hope again." Can you feel the difference in how your body registers your request for well-being and trust? When you speak to what is missing behind the numbness, you expose the nerve to the air. You discover that you are not in fact numb; you are suffering and crying out for solace.

(Listen to this audio meditation at sarahblondin.com/heart-minded-meditations)

PRACTICE Finding Your Heart at Your Edge

Close your eyes and just arrive in this moment. Notice the sound of the room around you, the sound of my voice, your breath, the ground supporting you. Come into the present moment by looking for the sweet hum of energy in your fingers, in the life force surging through you. Again, I want you to leave your mind behind, and let yourself really arrive here, without your ideas, beliefs, stories, or wounds. Empty yourself and open your palms to the sky as a sign of relinquishing all of these things.

Hope is born from connection with ourselves. It is born when we come down into the body to hear our spirit's requests.

Touch the heart now, feeling the raw edge of your hopelessness without fearing it, and invite yourself to stand at the edge with it.

Stand beside any despair or heartache you may be carrying with you at the edge of a cliff. A valley is stretching out before you and there is no one around but you and your longing.

Claim what you need now; speak your deepest desires out into the great unknown. What is it that you need most, dear one? Ask yourself. Is it safety? Faith? Trust? Or is it unconditional love and support? It could be relief or courage. Maybe you need to feel soothed, to know you are okay, that you are exactly where you need to be. From your own mouth, speak. Let yourself be heard.

Find your needs and focus your attention softly on your heart center; stay open to the wide unknown before you. Ask your inner self, your heart, if there is anything that needs your attention — anything you need to look at that maybe you are not.

Wait in quiet and receptive presence. See if you can hear a voice answering you. Sometimes our sweet heart does not use words, but flushes through us with warmth and waves of goosebumps as a way to make us feel heard and to make our hearts sing again. Feel for your heart's recognition or any words or insights coming to you from the ether. If nothing comes, just stand at the edge, awake and in awareness, simply enjoying this honest moment.

This is what it looks like to make space for your sweet heart to speak. Healing is available at every moment if we invite it, if we ask, if we listen, if we allow ourselves to feel our soreness. It is always there at your edge, dear one, waiting to wash away the debris.

In many shamanic societies, if you came to a shaman or medicine person complaining of being disheartened, dispirited, or depressed, they would ask one of four questions. When did you stop dancing? When did you stop singing? When did you stop being enchanted by stories? When did you stop finding comfort in the sweet territory of silence?

I'd like you to continue forward now, setting in place some sort of daily practice where you name what you need. Remember how to dance beside your struggles, remember how to sing your pain to sleep, remember how to find refuge in silence.

When you begin to feel the weight on top of your heart or the numbness creeping in, accept the invitation for growth and expansion; step out from the freight and inertia and shake your love awake. This will help in healing the waters of this earth, this will help you see the goodness beyond the small shouting parts. This will help in moving you through your pain and into the grace that's blooming on the other side.

You can open your eyes now.

Congratulate yourself for living awake. You see, even when you think you're numb, you are very much alive.

15

COMFORT FOR DEEP SUFFERING

The tide will begin to shift in response to the cry of a million unheard voices within you.

As you lose your appetite for blame, fear, and pain, you will begin to slowly lean toward the light.

Begin lifting your gaze toward the sky. Notice breath more often. Land in the space between thoughts.

Weight you have been carrying will fall to the earth at your feet and a robust feeling of hope and lightness will begin to spread out from your center, filling cracks and clefts. If you are caught back in the dark, you will be able to impel yourself up and out from these places of suffering more quickly.

Light has been busy threading itself through your darkness. You will feel this as a subtle birth of acceptance and a deep peace where there was none before.

You will, after tasting the great love at your center, learn to trust all that you are, at first slowly, then more and more fiercely.

As you begin choosing the things that bring you closer to love, you will still come face-to-face with stagnant waters within you. You will need to wade through some murky darkness to find more light.

You must hold true and continue forward. The most painful realization you will face is that there is still this abandoned part of you: your softness. Once touched, it will open an ache like no other. Do not let the magnitude of this feeling frighten you away. You are simply coming to learn that you have left a part of yourself behind. It will feel as though you are being reunited with a long-lost twin or kindred spirit; wildly tender yet central for your return to wholeness.

Now that you're in touch with your softness, you are born anew. As with all births, there is an aggressive churning of energies, a mounting pressure, and a final release. As long as you remain firm in your decision to live in harmony with your heart and true nature, you will be carried through the turbulent phase of birth with grace. This will not be the last birth. You will endure many births in your lifetime. All are for your highest good.

Do not be afraid of the great forces living within you. You are growing into your most wildly powerful self. What you are experiencing is a storm of great, great beauty. Let nothing convince you back into your smallness, for you are now moving toward your highest potential.

A LETTER FROM THE UNIVERSE

I am not immune to the hungry shadow of the dark that wanders on wind through the empty night—looking to feed on something soft.

I am not immune to the unease that burrows deep and hides each crumb of goodness from my weary sight.

But I am also not immune to the light building in force around that which has grown dim.

I am not immune to the fierce gusts of grace that come to knock claw and hook from marrow and rank.

I am not immune to the dark, but neither am I immune to the benevolence and beauty tirelessly working to set me free.

Often, when we initiate connection with our hearts, we are not prepared for the wild ride. We can be blindsided both by the magnitude of love revealed to us *and* by the riotous uproar of fear that can come screaming from doors we were sure we had locked forever. That's why it's so important that when we enter communion with this wise heart, we are prepared to surrender our defenses and to trust what belches forth from the shadows. Whether what comes forth in any moment is prodigious love or heavy-handed grief, our heart will guide us and teach us how to heal the wounds that have kept us from being fully heart minded.

Becoming heart minded is a tiered journey. We will be born into many levels of understanding, sometimes through a labor that involves an excruciating breakdown of our controlled minds and neat realities. The reward, of course, is arriving at a new plateau of love and revelation.

We must endure the dismantling of all that is holding us separate from our heart. Again and again, we will be asked to rise, to be reborn into greater love. Not one of us is immune to the hungry shadow of the dark.

Now, we are going to bring forward our darkness and give it the warmth of our attention. We have much to learn from our shadow realms—more, in fact, than from our light. In order to come into harmony and partnership with our full intelligence, it's important that we listen to what hurts. The fierce, untamed, and searing pain of the parts of ourselves we have lost or disowned speaks to us as panic and anxiety, depression and inertia. These need our loving attention if we are ever to come into proper alignment.

Think about a tree. When you look at a tree, you often only see flowers, leaves, and a thick, solid trunk. But there is another part that we don't see, a part burrowed deep into the earth that's entwined with stone and grit. Below the surface lives an intricate system of roots nimbly reaching toward things that help the tree grow, an intricate web of life living out of sight and in complete darkness. This is where the tree gathers all its sustenance. There would be no tree, no buds or bloom, were it not for the dark earth wrapping tight around half of its body.

Just like the tree, we grow half on the surface and half beneath it. But unlike the tree, we are immensely afraid of this darkness. This palpable fear is what causes us to disown, ignore, and shun half of who we are.

What does this say of our relationship with our very root? It says we only pray for bloom, neglecting the fact that there is no bloom without root and darkness.

Only good can come
from stretching your roots
further through stone and silt.
It is how you find nutrients
for the crown of leaves
you are soon to wear.

When we travel into the underworld and into our own opaqueness, it may not be enough to name a feeling and let it pass through. Sometimes the pain is more nebulous than a feeling. When we are in the terrain of panic, anxiety, depression, and high stress (which I would call high fear), we are being shown that we need to birth a greater awareness. We need to learn how to hold on to our hearts in the dark. This holding does not mean gripping, it means surrendering. It means opening wide against our instinct to tuck in tight and shield. We don't need protection in this place, we need grace, and in order to find this grace we need to learn to sit in hard places—to stay and wave our white flag of surrender—while also claiming our fierceness.

PRACTICE   Calling on Fierce

(Listen to this audio meditation at sarahblondin.com/heart-minded-meditations)

They say that a snake will die if it does not shed its skin. That if it holds on too long, the old skin will bond to the snake's body like glue and suffocate it. The same is so for us. If we don't learn to shed our old skin, if we try to hold on too dearly to what was, we risk death of spirit and self.

Though shedding and growth are inevitable, we tend to resist. Dread will often keep us grasping on. Then, the body, out of confusion, begins to malfunction. When we hold on too tight, our natural system chokes and we lose our sense of ground, body, the physical healing powers of breath, and the nurturing drum of our hearts.

When you have reached a place where a great trembling runs the length of your body, a trembling so strong you feel you are not able to put one foot in front of the other, know that you, my dear one, have come to a growth point. The person you have been up until now simply cannot carry you through to the other side. You must step boldly into this more expanded self. You must shed your skin.

You do not have to be afraid. It is your spirit, dear one, that has brought you to face this. Brought you to the doorway of your own expansion. You must push through the hard crust of your resistance.

Close your eyes and bring yourself to the door of your own mercy. Let your fear stand beside you. Likewise, your panic and your exhaustion. Let them be without judgment or fuss, and let your body do what it does best. Breathe.

Place both your hands gently atop your heart.

Bowing your head gently toward your chest and heart, give thanks for every aspect of your experience, for it is in giving thanks that we see clearly the gifts hidden in even the darkest crevices.

> *I thank you, dark nights, for you taught me to see that the dark is punctured by stars of light.*
>
> *I thank you, fear, for you revealed to me my inherent courage and strength.*
>
> *I thank you, each aching part, for you revealed to me my inherent powers to heal and love what felt impossible to love.*
>
> *I thank you, desperate cries for help, for you revealed to me my voice, and my longing for truth and awakening.*
>
> *I thank you, all of you …*

With your eyes still closed, rise now to your feet. Lift your face up to the sky in surrender to the mystery. Feel your feet firmly grounded on this earth, in this body, in this very moment. With one hand still on your heart, lift the other hand above your head in victory. Imagine it like a blade, cutting through the darkness. This is what your fierceness looks like when your heart is your anchor. The body and face in soft surrender and wonder while wielding a resolute clarity and determination.

It is time for you to become fierce. You must declare ownership of your being. You must roar in the face of even the darkest night, announcing that you believe in yourself, that no storm will quell your light; announcing that though your flame may be quivering, you nevertheless hold it high above your head.

Now, see yourself stretching beyond your usual limits. Announce that you are willing to move ahead, to answer the calls of growth. Announce that you are willing. Do not cower from the fear; do not run. It is time now, to roar.

As you claim your mighty spirit, you will lighten the dark. As you hear your own voice declaring ownership, you make your belief in yourself a reality. And the longer you stand on sure feet, the more your light will strengthen and widen around you.

It's time for praise, dear one. Praise your journey of discovery and reunion with what and who you are and are becoming. Praise. This is how you vote for your light.

You may release your pose now and rest. Open your eyes if you'd like.

Use this pose whenever you feel you are being asked to grow. Stand as a beacon of truth, stepping through the fire of your distrust. Believe, dear one, that you are so capable of this. Believe and it shall be.

Courage, beloved.

16

YOUR PAIN IS VALID

One of the things we learn as children is to avoid pain at all costs. And so we grow into adulthood often willing to go to the most extraordinary lengths to numb ourselves or deny that we hurt. It's time to clear up this misunderstanding and confusion once and for all.

Your pain is valid.

You may feel angry that love was not given nor modeled for you. You may feel helpless at confronting, or simply standing alongside, the angst and unrest within you. There is nothing wrong with your pain. It is sad, yes. Heartbreaking, of course. But it is not devastating. Nothing is capable of devastating you.

You are not a tumbleweed, dear one. You have agency. It's time to let go of your attachment to your hurt. To work your muscle of your love of the self and realign with the one true heartbeat of life. Hold your heart and self as sacred and dear. Even when under an attack of the spirit, you are so close to becoming free! If you are wise, you will take these moments of suffering as opportunities to pull more of yourself into truth and alignment. This means not distancing yourself from feeling, and instead staying in the very center of it and strengthening the muscles that will help you stand there in your highest knowing.

PRACTICE Calling on Grace and Kindness

(Listen to this audio meditation at sarahblondin.com/heart-minded-meditations)

Look down at your hands, my dear one; study the body that is you. Place them atop your heart. Close your eyes. Stay a while.

May I remind you that you are the owner of this home. This is your land, your garden, your earth, your kingdom. All that lives within you can be tended to by the great powers of your love.

You mustn't forget the wisdom that is yours. Hidden in the folds of your distrust, there is a power that you are learning to claim now. There is no hurt or wound that you cannot love, that you cannot smooth and soothe. This is your land, my dearest one.

Look inside yourself for the benevolent force that has been calling from the instant you could hear. From the moment you took those first tiny steps away from yourself, it has been here, attached to you by a thread of gold — your umbilical cord to the divine.

The more you inhabit your home, the more this cord strengthens and reties itself to the love you are made of.

You must invite the divine in you to hold you, to let it call you back and to open your senses to this wind of love, breathing from the quiet of your own being.

We all forget, but by grace, love, and earnestness we recover from this forgetfulness. You recover by simply becoming as still as you are now, no matter what is happening in your life and in yourself. By no longer turning away from every scab or scar, you learn to bond yourself to your own wisdom and heart.

Breathing now, gently, let the words *I am willing, I am allowing, I am opening, I am surrendering my defenses* wash through and over you. Let yourself be pulled closer to your own heart and away from your torment.

Can you now introduce kindness to whatever state you are in? What does kindness look like, dear one? Find a memory of this, or just a feeling. It may be a soft touch, it may feel like being heard or held, comforted or encouraged. Whatever this kindness looks like, let it spread over you. Let this kindness take and put down your fears and the worry or grief you are holding; let this kindness embrace you.

I am all right. I am okay.
You are all right. You are okay.

Now bring forward an image of grace. What does grace look like, dear one? Does it look like forgiveness? Or peace? Does it look like calm or letting go? Or does grace feel like spontaneous gratitude? Does it make your heart feel open? Or does grace look like the face of someone who was always happy to see you?

Let whatever grace looks like to you register in your loving awareness. Offer it to yourself, without condition or resistance. Let it heal what needs healing in you.

You are worthy of this grace. It has been waiting and trying to get through to you, waiting for you to summon it forward.

Your pain is valid, dear one, but not devastating, for you hold all the powers of healing you need. No one else can do this for you.

We are calling out for help, and we are the ones who must answer our own calls.

Opening your eyes now, be at peace.

17

TENDERIZING PAIN

Those of us most in pain are the ones who have not allowed it to be expressed in the safe circle of our own company. We then try to inflict our pain on others, but pain inflicted is pain expressed poorly. We express pain properly by holding it in love. This tenderizes it. Not only does it not spread outward, it no longer hurts so badly.

Why do I keep talking about pain? Life is more than pain, isn't it? Yes, of course it is. But we spend so much of life trying to hide from our shadow, and it's time to give it our loving attention.

We are all in pain. I am in pain. I see pain in my children, even though they're very young, and I see pain in my loved ones, especially in their compulsive need to control and oversee everything.

I see pain in all of us.

Again, this is not to say I don't also see tremendous love and joyful expression—that part is natural and easily given—but our pain parts are asking for liberation, and there is much to be reckoned with.

We feed our pain and allow it to fester and rot through avoidance. Becoming heart minded requires us to evolve out of our pain, and every one of us can do this if we are awake enough to let ourselves see every facet of who we are. Once we are willing to move into awareness, we awaken a mysterious world of spontaneous healing, revolutionary compassion, radical self-forgiveness, and perhaps the most important quality—deep caring.

PRACTICE   Pain as a Portal to the Divine
(Listen to this audio meditation at sarahblondin.com/heart-minded-meditations)

To reconnect with our deeply caring selves, we must slow to a stop. We must slow to a stop and connect with the earth breathing beneath our feet and the air that is life passing through us. So, let us close our eyes, and land in the moment, in the now, and focus on our breath.

Sometimes when we are in deep suffering, we might wish for life to come to an end. This feeling, though it sometimes feels like disdain for our life, is not that at all. It is a call to reconnect with our hearts. We must be careful not to focus solely on what is hurting within us, for you are alive and well under this pain, alive and in love with your beating heart.

I want you to bring an in-pain part of you forward. It can be a memory or something going on for you right now — even a physical pain. Believe me when I say this pain can become your portal to the divine. You must learn to see it as a kindness, an offering, an outstretched palm guiding you to healing water.

A wise woman named Ruby Sales taught me to ask the question: Where does it hurt?

So tell me, dear one, where does it hurt in you?

Feel the ache of all the unaddressed discomfort, shame, lingering sadness, and general malaise that sometimes comes with being alive. Let yourself meet it, not avoid it. Let yourself be okay with not being okay for right now. Let whatever it is be in you, without condition.

Now, look at this ache and begin to awaken a sort of pleasure response. Take a big inhale and let out a deep sigh. Hear and feel the sound of that sigh.

Notice how it brings a relief and a type of grace that wraps itself around your suffering.

Now, placing a hand on your heart, begin to gently sway, rocking yourself as you would a new babe. We are still staying with our pain, but now we are tenderizing it. Once the edges of your pain soften, let them slip down and away from you. Drop them from your arms, your thoughts, your mind. Let them become impersonal. There is no need to keep holding them or to pick them back up.

These sweeping waves of pain and heartache are very real feelings, but they are not who you are. They are but wind passing and waves crashing on the shore of your great beauty. Keep rocking yourself gently, evoking joy even in this challenge. You are alive. This, too, is a gift. You and all your weather are in some way a blessing disguised. It brings you close to source, if you are willing to receive in the midst of it.

Recognize that feeling in any form is a gift. We are lucky to feel so deeply, for behind each feeling, even the hard ones, is love. We hurt because we love so deeply.

Your suffering is not despair, dear one, but desire: desire to meet the divine within you, desire to know your great strength.

You are alive and well, dear one; under the chaos, you are alive and in love with your beating heart. When suffering comes, know it is your own self-love you are lonely for.

You are trying to awaken your capacity to care for your own life and self. Do not be fooled by the voices of your discontent. Let yourself be wise to the needs that lurk behind the guise of those voices. It is always love asking to be seen, always love asking to be held.

Open your eyes, still holding yourself with warmth. Be wise in your power by introducing the sigh of grace and your potent loving presence to everything that asks. This is how you tenderize your pain.

18

COMMITMENT TO
WHAT IS GOOD

This isn't easy—this eruption after eruption that happens as we venture toward heart mindedness. This burgeoning life of yours—it is not easy. You are learning to see in the dark. Learning to walk with no one there to hold your hand. Learning to give to yourself what was not given to you in times when you needed it most. Learning to choose love, when you are yourself just slowly learning to uncover it.

This isn't easy, dear one—this facing yourself, choosing not to turn away from your life. It is not easy to see where your feet are stuck in mud and to be in the place of stubborn, repeated pattern and pain. It isn't easy to witness how you disempower yourself, the places you wish someone else could heal for you. It is not easy to keep strong and soft and gentle in the face of your continued learning and exposing.

It's not easy, dear one. I know it is not easy. But perhaps it can be. If we see life through the clarity of our heart we do not see struggle. As we've begun to see, beauty is not beautiful without the shadow cast by the darkness, by the hard. Contrast is life; life is contrast. Our heart-minded self loves all.

We cannot rid ourselves of one and not the other, so there is only one choice, and that is to love the faces of the shadow and the unexpected.

If it is your desire to open to your life, you must commit to tending to what is good and true within you. You must look upon your inner garden, kneeling within to tend lovingly to your earth, pulling out weed and rot, and showing up regardless of thundering storm or weather in order to coax what is beautiful up from the soil.

PRACTICE   Voting for the Heart
(Listen to this audio meditation at sarahblondin.com/heart-minded-meditations)

The heart can still beat amidst fear and paralyzing thoughts. A cancer can grow unnoticed in a body while the hands paint pictures, write poetry, and make love. While wars are being fought, mothers still dress their children for school.

Opposite things often live beside one another.

We suffer, but still we must learn to commit to standing alongside all suffering, with a presence that says, *I am here, without condition.* Though the pain is deep and fatigue tries to pull us back to sleep, we must rise. Still we must commit to what is good and true.

As long as you keep choosing to give tender attention and devotion to your inner world, you are doing what you can to grow what matters most. Whatever is hard now stands beside the most soft and loving. What is afraid stands beside what is fearless.

Closing your eyes now, notice if anything is hurting inside you. Notice anything you may want to avoid or react negatively toward. Notice anything that feels calloused or simply not at rest or in peace. Let it be there, without judgment. Let it dance its dance around you for a moment.

Now, shift your attention to feel your breath rising and falling. Feel the natural engine operating in favor of your life. How your breath comes as a form of grace and gentle companionship. How the air offers calm. How the quiet of the room reaches out to you. See that you are standing beside what is hard but also what is gentle and quiet.

You, in this moment, have agreed to vote for your heart. Agreed to be courageous in your loving and in your nurturing of your true self. By being here in this moment, dear one, you are agreeing not to be afraid, to learn of your fearlessness and compassion for your life. You are voting for the heart within you, for the goodness you are most yearning for.

Yes, your pain is still here with you, but you have not run. You have arrived fully to take care of goodness and truth. This is what courage looks like.

Courage is not screaming angry words in empty rooms; it is calming this impulse and then stepping into the opposite world right beside it. By surrendering from the fight, even just in this moment, you create within yourself a refuge beside the unbearable.

You are voting, dear one, for what is true. Though the fear and fury will rise, still you arrive to feed what is most true, sitting here gently beside them.

It is not easy, dear one, to guide yourself in the direction of love's great light, but you are learning. You are brilliant in your efforts and it does get easier. Trust that your body, your innermost intelligence, already knows how to lead you there. Be gentle; befriend the many faces that come to knock at your door. Let all of your life's lessons illuminate, not grip. Let them arrive light as feathers, dipped in grace.

Open your eyes. You have committed to being the safe place where all may land; let no unrest cause you to forget this promise. There is in each moment the choice to deepen your commitment, to stand for what you most long for, to commit to what is good, and to vote, dear one, for your heart.

PART 3
HEART-MINDED INTIMACY

This
Sky
Where we live
Is no place to lose your wings
So love, love,
Love.

HAFIZ, *I HEARD GOD LAUGHING*

As we explore the liberating power of our heart, we are learning a more open way to look at our self and our experience. We can begin to recognize what it means to live in a heart-minded way and to see our role in choosing to awaken and stay awake in our heart. The more we allow the heart to touch us, the more we feel fulfilled and satisfied and the more meaningful our life becomes.

While we have on some level already been dealing with how to live heart mindedly in our relationships, this next section specifically focuses on how to be in our heart with the ones we love most.

Being in our heart will involve putting into action our commitment to serve our heart-minded nature. Our relationships help us learn experientially, not just conceptually, how to practice choosing our heart. Relationships give us the invaluable gift of assisting us in strengthening our devotion, our understanding, and our action in the name of love.

19

LETTING GO OF
CONDITIONAL LOVE

You are built from this ancient, wild earth. You breathe the same air as all life that has ever been in existence. You are as mighty as any force that stands beside you. You will begin to truly understand this the deeper you travel into the realms of your internal world. The further you reach within, the wider your understandings and perceptions of the world and who you are in essence will become.

Joy will rise, flushing out old stagnant beliefs and structures. Joy will spill out from your heart center and sever your ties with all binding relationships, patterns, and thoughts. It will leave no room for that which suffocates the beauty of your being; it will leave no room for behavior that steals life from you or those around you.

As your emblazoning continues, space will begin to empty around you. Your closed thinking and hurtful thoughts will quiet to whispers and then disappear almost entirely. They will no longer hold the attraction they once did. If they visit again, you will know not to feed them for nothing is worth the devastation of your joy. You know that you are larger than all the thoughts that keep you and the life around you small. You have expanded beyond the ordinary and have entered into a field of freedom.

You have encountered the stormy waters of your life and have been born into a new understanding. You have turned toward the fear held within you and have in turn been given a fearless heart. You have seen that there, beyond the fault-finding, is a world of delight and ease.

Great beauty will reveal itself to you in the plain, simple, and ordinary life you get to live as you begin to set yourself free—from bondage, from fear, from your small frames of focus.

Any indifference to your life will die away. You will stand bare and emptied. You will stand on the earth, heart alive, hands open, whispering to the divine winds that brush against you, *I am here, and I care. I am here, and I care.*

All of life will dance before you in a wild symphony of delight. It will recognize your long journey, your valiant effort, and give to you the gift of a life being fully lived.

A LETTER FROM THE UNIVERSE

Often the most painful experience we have as humans is the learning we reap through loving another.

When we commit to love, a ripening and deepening of the soul begins. But with this invaluable gift comes a sort of breaking of internal ground. The ones closest to us trigger, mirror, ignite, and reveal both our great beauty and great ugliness. To attempt love is to also suffer an honest revealing of our darkest tendencies and selves.

If we have the intention, as most of us hopefully do, to discover the greatest amount of love we can in this lifetime, we must allow an intimate other to guide us to our blind spots, our most brittle and lacking-of-love places. Once we are brought to the place where we are surprised and humbled by our unloving behavior, we can begin the good work. The work that helps us restabilize and realign our systems and selves with purity of heart.

It was far easier for me to learn to love myself, to become heart minded, when dealing with my private, inner struggles than it was in my intimate relationships. I always had a hard time being loving if my conditions were not being met. *Treat me this way and I will open up and love you. Behave well and only then will I reciprocate.* I genuinely wanted to live in my heart, but I realized I had this impossibly stubborn part of me holding everyone I loved at arm's length and under a strict conditional love agreement.

This conditional way of loving in relationships acts as a hindrance to love. For us to truly become heart minded, we need to find a way to not act out from this stubborn, indignant aspect of ourselves.

To soften in the face of betrayal or disappointment or hurt seems as dramatic as inviting someone who has just punched you in the gut into your home for a cup of warm tea. When we are triggered in love, this seems like an entirely impossible proposal.

So how do we do this? How, when we have been hurt or betrayed or wounded by another, can we open our hearts?

The answer is: practice. We practice offering some small vulnerability in the face of our habits of hostility and closing. When we are at the edge, and we feel ourselves being pushed to rage against or lock out someone we love, we must activate our true nature instead. What can we offer from a place of compassion and strength, from clarity and intelligence? What can we offer to our experience in truth and love?

I am feeling angry. I don't know how to choose love right now. I am afraid to be hurt. I am afraid to love.

We don't have to surrender completely; we just have to leave the door of our hearts ajar so love has a way to get through.

In the act of giving voice to our fears and uneasiness, we are opening the door for compassion and the possibility of healing. The first word offered that carries the sweet softness of heart is often the hardest word to speak, but once done, once carried out on breath and felt by and in the heart, it will unleash a torrent of love. A windfall comes, like a dam whose walls have broken, to heal and fill the lacking gaps and wounds. This courageous behavior leaves an indelible imprint on us that is necessary for the essential activation of our hearts. The reward does not come from the response of the other—their actions cannot be guaranteed—but from our own awakening and choosing to love regardless of the conditions.

After leading a meditation for a group on retreat, I was approached by someone who wanted to know how I am able to let my heart remain open. She had suffered tremendously from an abusive mother as a little girl. Each time she would try and let herself open her heart in meditation, she would feel this paralyzing resistance to it. This deeply afraid part of her would scream "No!" each time she would try. She wanted to live from her heart but could not figure out how to stop this deep resistance against loving.

I explained to her that I too had had that voice inside myself. Having grown up terrified by life and getting hurt by the actions of those I most loved, I had also struggled to let love in.

I told her I had spent years fighting to protect my heart. I would eventually begin to see each person I fell in love with as my enemy. In conflicts, I fought brutally and relentlessly and then would flee and withdraw. When I would meet anyone new, I would judge and criticize their character because it would help me feel less vulnerable to the possibility of being hurt by them. When I did try to love someone, I would always wait for the other shoe to drop, always wait for the fallout. This is what battling *against* the heart looks like. These actions were my way of trying to stand up for my heart, when really all they were doing was causing me to *steep* in heartache.

I recounted to her a time when I was storming through the forest, after my hundredth fight with my partner, when something pivotal shifted inside me. In the midst of my rage, my heart miraculously opened. I stopped in my tracks and fell to my knees on the earth and cried. I was overwhelmed by feeling the sheer power of my heart surging through me. It tore down my indignation and self-righteousness.

I could no longer see my lover as wrong or even separate from me. The war inside me had stopped. The radiant energy of the heart engulfed me. I went straight home and hugged my beloved, letting every part of my being open in his arms. I felt the energy radiating from my heart begin to open his heart. It was as though, in that moment, we merged together and became one beaming orb of love. Unrestrained love. This. This is what I wanted. This was what I had been looking for. This love is what I wanted to feel always.

In that experience, I saw that the heart was not breakable, but indestructible and always there to help us in our struggles.

Everything changed for me. I could never un-feel or forget the power of my heart. I had tasted what it was to become infused with the heart and I wanted nothing more than to feel that in every moment of my life and for every person, even if they were not acting in accordance with my desires. I saw that if I opened my heart completely, I was capable of manifesting, creating, instigating, encouraging, and invoking love. If I was completely open in my heart, I was making love possible, not impossible.

I explained to this woman that whatever she thinks people may try to take from her cannot be taken. This love, this heart we spend so much time and energy protecting, can never be harmed or stolen. It is a renewable resource. We are wasting our time in protecting it; it is ours and always will be.

Something in what I said registered as truth in her. She said she felt lighter, relieved. The story from my heart began to open her heart, and both our beings entered the comfort of an open-hearted exchange.

We are not here to be separate and alone in our lives. Love and kindness is what heals and bonds us to the world around us. Our challenge is to be a careful witness to all of the ways we protect ourselves from loving. To look for all of the ways we start to numb ourselves with judgmental barriers and hurtful stories that pull us closed and cause us to be alone with ourselves.

We can do this by noticing the first sign of our tightening and closing against someone or something. When we feel threatened, a quickening of energy begins inside our body. This can feel like tightening in our chest, throat, or stomach. These constrictive sensations, shallow and short breathing, and hurtful repeated thoughts mean your system is suffering. Greatly suffering. It means you are not in the flow and generosity of life; it means you are being held captive by your judgmental, critical, and unloving self.

Self-preservation, the inability to choose softness in the face of your hurt, is a self-imposed prison.

Our fight-or-flight instinct is being activated in these times of distress. Unwittingly, we are using this inborn instinct, which is meant to protect us from dangerous predators, against the ones we love. But here's the thing. We are at liberty to make a different choice. So, notice when you try to push off and away to your safe island. Come back to the moment or the person in front of you and challenge yourself to stay instead.

Dig beneath the thick and wild anger and fear to find your intention: *to embody your heart and stand as love.*

Learn to slow the momentum of judgments and critical thoughts by bringing their short, fearful movements into a relaxed, drawn out, conscious breath. This is how you step down from the storm of the mind and arrive within yourself. Awake. Aware. Witnessing.

You need only a crack of softness to be broken open. To be supported by love's divine grace and virtuosity, you need make only the smallest gesture in the direction of heart.

Then, hold yourself with gentle compassion. We only feel the need to fight or flee when we are very much afraid. So, you must lovingly tell this self that you are all right.

Invite your heart to heal and soothe even the greatest fear within you.

This does not mean you must accept the wrongdoings of others if you are being hurt and harmed, but it means you are committing to engaging and acting from the perspective of loving awareness. You are committed to calmly and lovingly addressing the other. You will remove yourself from the situation if you need to, but in peace, not in anger.

This is a practice of entering the heart. It is a muscle you must learn to work if you deeply desire a heart-minded life.

The sooner you can hand something over to love, the sooner your pain will be relieved. The burden is no longer yours alone to carry. Those pains we keep knotted over our hearts are what stop us from being fully alive. The more fulfilling life we all thirst for is found in relinquishing our pain and handing it over to be healed by the redemptive power of love.

Those still caught in reactive, uncompassionate behaviors will always be a part of our lives, and at times, we too will be this person in someone else's life. The only thing you have real control over is how you respond and resolve the issue. When you refuse to react or run from the situation and instead ground yourself in your love and kindness, you create a new set point in your mind that says: Hold in love. Trust in love.

Hold yourself in love, hold others in love, and hold out, as you wait for the storm to calm, in love.

Trust in love.

Trust that each person wants to be their true nature of love. Trust that each person is longing for direction and examples of healthy, loving people. *Be* that example. Trust that as long as you have built and honored your love within, others will follow, others will respond, and you will help in changing your small corner of the world.

This is the good work. The real work. To become infused with love's light and then stand as a beacon of hope for others looking for their way home.

20

THERE ARE NO WRONG CHOICES

In retrospect, dear one,
you will understand
your entire life was choices,
made one after another
in the name of love,
or preserving that love.

Nothing will be wrong or broken,
just choices made,
either way, in the name of your heart.

In the months leading up to my wedding day, a storm of incredible velocity swirled inside me. Fear and doubt screamed through my body and thoughts. Up until that point, I had made only small, insignificant commitments in my life. Fluidity and nonattachment had always made me feel more comfortable. Unconsciously, I believed that committing to something, anything, meant I would inevitably face failure, my failure.

Regardless of the clarity I felt when I said yes to marrying my now-husband, I wrestled with my incredibly fierce and fearful predilection to avoid anything that could cause me pain.

Another part of me though—my heart—kept urging me to trust the process and the unfolding.

Luckily, I followed my heart and chose love. Chose to love him. I say luckily because carrying through with marrying him ignited a process of growth within me that would have never been possible had I continued staying detached and living only on the surface. He continues to help me see where it is I am most afraid, where I choose to wage war, and the lonely places within me that are unavailable to love.

Though we have faced unpleasant seasons in our relationship, we have learned how to choose and create harmony. We lead each other to our blind spots, and we use these revelations to address the old buildup of our hurt. We work at opening to each other, even when angry, with a willingness to really see and hear one another. We are each other's sacred tools. We help each other evolve.

We've been married eight years now. I know we make each other better people. We've brought two sweet ones into the world and created a beautiful home and existence that's surrounded by nature, and yet, under the tremendous beauty of all we have, the voice of doubt still comes:

How will we survive life after children?

Will we find our way back to one another?

We are so different.

Maybe we are better suited with someone else.

Fear, still standing there like a wall of fire trying to keep me safe from the pain that may come one day . . . or may not. This voice stops me from living completely with an open heart. While we may think these voices protect us, they create distance between us and our choices and make some part of us unavailable to love.

One day a while back, my husband and I had a particularly aggressive disagreement, and I went to a quiet room to meet the pain of my inflexibility. I slowed, I breathed, I chose to arrive in front of the unpleasant feeling standing between me and my heart. Placing my hand on my heart, I asked the deepest part of me what it was I was needing to hear most in this place of uneasiness. An answer draped around me like a cashmere blanket: there is no such thing as a wrong choice.

Hearing this, every inch of my body softened. A clenching feeling I was holding for what seemed like years suddenly released. And then I saw it: the buried fear of "making the wrong choice," the buried fear of my failure. Every time there was a conflict between my husband and me, it would scream: "See! There it is! You were right not to submit entirely to him! I knew it! Thank god you didn't fully trust. Thank god you didn't fully love!"

This voice, this worry, this belief was operating underneath the surface of the most precious relationship of my life. Like a tap left on, slowly draining the beauty of our union.

My heart helped me recognize this voice of sabotage and instilled faith and trust in its place. It said that even if all my fears prove right, nothing—not one choice you have made in the name of love—will be wrong.

Each relationship, regardless of whether it "succeeds" or "fails," brings to us an understanding about ourselves that we never could have had otherwise. Relationships offer valuable and unique awakenings of our spirit. We may label them "negative" or "positive," but they are awakenings nonetheless. They bring about revelations. There is no need to create a boundary between you and those you hold dear. Much is given and learned by those who dare to love.

Waiting for the other shoe to drop, waiting for our lover to abandon us, waiting for our confirmation that, yes, in fact we did make the wrong choice, is like holding our breath underwater. It is deciding that love is destined to fail us. It holds everyone we love at a distance. The consequence of this belief is that it becomes too easy to close ourselves off from those we most love and to create friction and war with one another. The quality of our life suffers and we become less available to love.

When you notice that you are feeling anger or discomfort with a loved one, or discomfort with an employee or friend, instead of turning away, look for the light behind your annoyance. Discover the truth that is trying to come forward by asking yourself:

> *Why am I choosing to create dissonance with*
> *this person, and in turn, myself? Why am I*
> *refusing to love? What am I refusing to feel?*

You may hear:

> *I am afraid I will not be loved.*

> *I am afraid I will be abandoned, that I am not good*
> *enough, that they will steal my love from me.*

> *I fear life. I am afraid that life is not kind. That*
> *if I do not fight, I will become a victim to great*
> *harm. That I will never mend. That once damage*
> *has been done, I will not be able to be repaired.*

> *I am weak, fragile. I lack worth. I am not deserving*
> *of love.*

These voices sit in front of our heart. They stand like tyrants in protection of our tenderness. In the moments when we are in true alignment with our heart, these voices do not speak. These voices hold no power. When we are in our heart, we know we are made of love, we forgive and release those we are in conflict with, we let go of the hurt, we reenter harmony and love. On the other side of these voices is our truth. The opposite of what they are saying is reality:

I am love. It is never lacking or able to be stolen from me.

I am good enough. I trust life. Life is kind. There is no pain too great not to be fed by my love and kindness.

I am strong. My worth is not to be gained. I am already all of the worth I will ever be.

By coming into awareness and understanding, you stop living your life fearing love. The light you ignite within yourself when you are in your heart begins to heal and ends painful patterns of defensiveness and battle. You begin to set others free. You no longer attach in unhealthy ways, for you are standing in the power of your life-giving essence and source.

PRACTICE   Seed of Wholeness

(Listen to this audio meditation at sarahblondin.com/heart-minded-meditations)

Close your eyes and come to find rest, in your body, in your life, in this moment. Suspend all other duties and tasks. Your job in this moment is to let go.

Now breathe ... place one hand on your heart, the other on your belly ... breathe.

You were conceived as a whole and perfect seed. All you would ever need is nested in the very center of this seed, in the very center of you.

Imagine for me your body as this perfectly round and rich bulb of life.

Because each of us was instructed to venture out from this bulb, we reached away from our personal riches. We fractured away from our epicenter, our vital core. And our seed split and began to shred.

Imagine for me your body as this perfectly round and rich bulb of life that's now fragmented and tattered. In your quest for love, for respect, for worth, for adoration, for nourishment, a ribbon split off and away from your center. Each judgment made, each hurtful word said, each barrier built between you and others resulted in more ribbons.

Relationships can point us to where we split away from our loving origin and wholeness and entered lack and defense. Our relationships are our sacred tools, teaching us, if we are willing, how to bring the split-off and fractured threads of our being back to home and center.

They can lead us back to the abundance of our original seed.

When you feel your patterns of judgment begin to spark or anger flooding your body, envision your seed of wholeness. Do not compromise the health of this seed by reacting with malice or foreclosure but instead hear the voice of healing inside yourself.

The part of you that feels stubborn and unwilling to practice opening to love is the saddest, most lonely aspect of you. Be wise in what parts of yourself you are empowering with your behaviors and choices. Do not be complacent with your healing. Do not fall back into patterns of hurt. Stay in the seat of your perfection. Refuse to splinter from your wholeness. Hold true in who you really are.

Listen inside for the things you have been hoping to have confirmed by someone outside of you. Are you hoping to be told you are worthy? Are you hoping someone finally says you are good? Are you asking for respect and adoration?

Whatever you are asking from others you must give to yourself. Everything we demand from others is something we most need from ourselves.

From wholeness, we love. We ease and soothe the hearts of others. We give, we open, we empower, we feed, we nurture. We give life.

There is no need, dear one, to defend and rally against love, against others. You are a seed of perfect wholeness. It's time to remember that nothing can threaten this; it is who you are in truth.

None of our experiences are meant to be snapped away by our fingers or wished away on breath. They are meant to be lived in any way we choose. So, if love is what you wish to find, let others reveal to you where it is most barricaded.

Agree to dance with the faces you condemn and judge, the moments you seize in fear. Say, "Welcome, dearest strain around my heart. I am ready to see how to lift the veil from this place now."

This is how we move from victimhood into mighty and courageous selfhood.

There is no place to rest but in your own agreement to be human and to wade through both the beautiful and the frightening. If you so choose, my dear one, you can recognize that each thorn removed is a place where your light will escape and eventually overwhelm you in love.

Open your eyes now. Go forth now, remembering the image of your already-whole seed. When you stay rooted instead of splintering off, an insight never before revealed will fall like a ripe plum into your basket.

Your harvest of light and wisdom comes from relationships. Use them. Love them. And let them show you how to love yourself and this wondrous life.

21

WHEN WE HARM
INSTEAD OF LOVE

In the hardest moments of our humanness we hurt our most beloved ones. It will almost feel as though you are witnessing a lost part of yourself as you react in malice and judgment. You may wince at each blow and each word and action that's out of alignment with the love you are trying so hard to work toward. There will be devastating moments when you will break your own heart. It is hard to have wisdom, intention, and understanding and still behave in ways that hurt another life.

There's no more painful a place to stand than there: in the wake of your war, emptied and deeply ashamed of yourself. To hold yourself in love in these moments can challenge even the most well trained of us. If you have inflicted abuse onto another, then you too have suffered abuse. There is no separation between you and the external. You will feel your actions rippling through your very tissues. We are not separate.

The best you can do to repair this is to try, as best you can, to stay with yourself. Pain exposed, not tuned out or numbed with television or substance. Try instead to tenderly dress your wounded heart. Soak in a bath. Be still. Find quiet.

Invite each feeling of embarrassment and shame to sit alongside you.

You can push it deeper into the closets of your internal world, but there is no escaping it. You may find ways to dull the pain, but you will continue suffering long after the damage has been done so long as you do not address it.

I urge you to face your actions not later, but when you are most tender, most close to the surface. That's how you become free. This means unbarricading your heart. Letting your feelings speak loudly and clearly, doing their part to help ease along the process of healing. The closer you are to the painful experience, the more sharply you can hear everything.

While we often dislike this place because of the intensity of it, your body's intelligence is trying to begin the process of moving you toward your loving self.

After a fight or fallout, when you are most sensitive, you are also most in touch with your emotional intelligence. If allowed, it will naturally spill out of you. Give each stab of regret and shame a name and it will release.

Regret, hate, anger, disgust, hopelessness, fear . . . on and on, let them spill from you. Let your body do what it knows to do; let it create a comforting space for your healing. Then, once emptied, soak, sit, and wait. When something has caused us devastation, relief is not instant. Hold yourself gently. Do comforting things. Rest. Sleep if you need to.

There, in the sacred space you created around yourself, something beautiful begins to kindle. Without much effort on your part, your system begins to lace healing through your pain. You have purged and broken yourself open with honesty, you have let the mind run its circle, and now grace will do the rest. The memory and pain will loosen; things will lift. Love will fill the emptied parts. You have taken the steps needed for your freedom from prolonged suffering. Freedom may not come in an instant, either for you or the others involved, but it will come.

This is a process of moving toward love, a process of not getting lost from ourselves just because we caused hurt or experienced a momentary lapse of our own better judgment, our own loving nature.

Mastery of a skill is said to take ten thousand hours or more. With each hour that we hold our self and our healing as sacred, we come closer to the mastery of loving. What could be more valuable than choosing to continually challenge ourselves to love more, and more, and more. There is nothing more precious to witness than a person struggling to turn their agony into freedom.

The larger the struggle, the larger the insight at the end. The more painful, the more grace, compassion, and wisdom will be poured into your heart. You will be compensated for your efforts. Love leaves no holes. It will fill what you invite it to.

Love will pool around each eye and heart and hand you come to touch. It will no longer be hidden from you once you actively begin choosing to transform. By simply opening in honesty, you will be brought back to wholeness.

PRACTICE   A Prayer for Growth
(Listen to this audio meditation at sarahblondin.com/heart-minded-meditations)

Now close your eyes, let your jaw loosen and fall, and drop your shoulders down and away from your ears. Notice the comfort in being so soft, so boundless, so unrestricted. Breathe here for a moment in this vulnerable, yet nourishing place.

Take a moment to let the word *love* fill your heart center and travel out through your chest, down your arms and your legs, and up through the crown of your head. Let it spread its gifts through your whole being and into your cells. Thank it. Appreciate it. Ask for more.

A prayer for you, as you learn to stay with all that is brought to your attention, to stay with your many uncomfortable teachers and lessons:

> *Dear tender heart, may you find refuge in this moment from all that feels hard and tired within your mind. May you relax into the gift that is you.*
>
> *May you allow your heart to take the lead. May you stop choosing to close. May you remain seated in your vulnerability. May you remember that you are here in this place, with everything you meet, to experience love and its many faces. May you deepen your connection with the ones sitting before you.*
>
> *May you realign with your intention, the reasons you are in relationship. May you refuse to let your fear of pain cause you to stop choosing love or create distance from what you most long for.*
>
> *Dear tender heart, you are growing. Be gentle with your heart and with the hearts of those you love. Do not feed the anger creating separation between souls and spirit and self. Swallow the injustice you perceive and make a small offering of love in place of tension. Reveal one small vulnerability and watch as love comes to meet you.*

Exhale and rest. Take note, the greatest power lies in what you choose to call the tight, uncomfortable places. Choose instead to call these the places where love is opening to a whole new level of beauty.

Do not close. You are choosing growth over stagnation, love over pain. You are making an effort to align with what you most desire. No matter the outcome, whether you receive what you are looking for or not, feel the warmth and sincerity of your actions; know you are trying to become more whole in heart and being. Let that, in each moment, be good enough.

Rest with your heart outside its cage, nerves open to the air and light and healing presence of life. Do not shut yourself or your heart back in, for this is the surest way to harden the soul, which was given to you to be soft.

PART 4
THE HEART
OUTSIDE ITS CAGE

This, my dear one, is what you have been looking for.
You have become the gentle earth where all is welcome
to land. Where no visitor will be turned away or banished.
Where there will always be love.

When you are being your heart-minded self, it is bliss. The heart is open, the mind is clear, you are settled; there is no need for argument or war within you. You experience unity with your essential nature of love and kindness.

As you continue forward, you will gain deeper awareness and more awakenings and be asked to face a new place that will bring lessons you have yet to learn. We are forever evolving. To help support and encourage your ongoing exploration of the heart, this last practice will involve declaring your heart-minded intention to yourself and to the world. This will release you into the mercy, goodness, and grace of a heart-minded life.

22

THE AWAKENING:
A POEM ABOUT
HEART-MINDED SEEING

To my lover, my husband, my wife, my child, my dearest friend, my mentor. To the stranger I pass on the street, the kind eyes that meet mine, the gentle breath shared while being embraced. To the ear that listened and held my words as precious. To the ones who stand with me in this lifetime.

To the life that rises along with the sun, that opens my eyes, that floods my body with vitality and vigor. To the love that spills from light, the love that falls from the seams in my clothing, to the abundance that fills the cup of clean water I drink.

To the fighting, the warring, the violent storms that crash within me and around me, to the ones that come to help show what hurts in order to be healed. To the people who are on this healing journey with me who are not allowing me to stay small but are forcing growth to come bursting forth from the wound that binds us together.

To the remembering of who I am. To the glimpses of my formless beauty, my unstoried self. To the remembering and then forgetting again. To the cycle and circle and dance with essence

and all that is not. To the heartbeat of my humanity, the tenderness of learning to walk without hands to hold. To this gentle,
most incredible journey we are all on.

To the breaking free from our painful, conditional joy and
happiness to begin loving someone and needing nothing in
return. To the giving of yourself to the fires that come to burn
your restrictive walls to ash. To the coming home and leaving
and coming home again.

To the fear found in my clenched fist, my sore shoulders, my
shallow breath, the knot in my stomach. To the fear that seizes
the homes of the places within me that are not aligned with my
core self. To the fear that is there to remind me, relentlessly, of
the places where I need to open my eyes. The places within me
that I need to love, the places that made me forget who I was
before I learned to clench against it all.

To the dark nights, the relief of the moon. The soft earth
that forms to cradle the shape of my foot. To the crickets and
the birds who sing our world into harmony. To the flowers that
wish to sit on my windowsill, the trees that grow to reach the
most sunlight. To the grass that sways and soothes. To the webs
the spider tirelessly builds overnight only to be torn down in the
daylight. To the life that pulses in exaltation below my feet every
day that I am alive. To the portal it offers into a remembrance of
our wholeness. To our source of unconditional love.

To the beauty that comes from hitting the rocks at the
bottom of the well. To the surrender that comes after I have been
squeezed of my last drop of control. To the overwhelming freedom that lives there behind everything I diligently carry. To the
wealth that waits for me to turn my gaze toward it.

To the gift of letting go. To the outstretching of palms. To the
laying down of arms. To the miracles born from not doing but
being. To the unclaimed love we are all blundering toward. To

the gravitational pull that constantly tugs us toward center even when we are screaming in the other direction. To the constant unearthing of who we really are. To the waxing and waning, to the groaning and the roaring. To the discoveries that blaze. To our valiance, our fortitude, our constant learning.

To our courageous, beautiful selves. To the purity of who we are, the mighty force we were born as. To the vulnerable, most magnificent heart in our chest. To the world of wonder shrouded in every soul.

To the simple, the plain, the ordinary life I get to live: I would like to say, thank you. I would like to share my most sincere gratitude and love and appreciation.

To the simple, the plain, the ordinary life I get to live: I would like to say a most sincere thank you for all of this glory that waits for me to turn my gaze toward it. I thank you. I love you. I thank you.

Close your eyes. Let these recognitions be what you carry close as you rise and fall throughout your day. Let this anchor you to the love that is yours, that is waiting, that you are infused with.

Let yourself be reminded that everything is a gift—a raucous, riotous, astonishing gift for you to revel in. There is no right and wrong, no good and bad, no must be's. This is it. A tale of fervent love. A tale of how you learned to discover the immense beauty living inside you.

Breathe. Hold your heart. Take a deep inhale and exhale. Go forth, dearest love, into the great pilgrimage of your life and offer your most sincere thanks for all that is. For all of the glory that waits for you to turn your attention to it.

(Listen to this audio at sarahblondin.com/heart-minded-meditations)

23

SIT AWAKE BEFORE THE WORLD

Life will come as it does, in waves of great joy and great despair. It will come in wide spans of comfort and discomfort. But there, right in the middle of you, is a solid, unaffected presence. It is neutral, neither fazed by the good nor the bad days of your life. It is a sanctuary from the ever-changing current of "reality."

In the end, all you will truly be left with is how much peace you gained, how much peace you found within you. This peace will carry you through your life—no matter the praise, no matter the critics, no matter how the world takes form in front of you.

So, dearest one, sit awake before the world and before your own self. Witness and then act in accordance with what your spirit is seeing, your deep knowing. Practice growth and evolution in conscious ways. Wake in this sleeping crowd of slumbering hearts and stand as a blazing light of fire to help burn the darkness back and away.

Never stop the momentum of healing, turning over your hurts and hurdles until the ragged edges of the stone become smooth. Remember that glass—a smooth surface through which we can see clearly—begins as a grain of sand, which itself was humbly derived from a brazen, impenetrable, and mighty boulder that was ground down into small, soft stones over time.

Yes, life has its uncertainties, but you don't need to keep being drawn toward the frantic voices clamoring for land they have yet to find first within themselves. Step-by-step you can carve the path.

No matter the scenario, truth will find a way to speak. Listen, hush, quiet. You already know this in your heart of hearts; you have the power to surrender yourself to the gentle current of life.

To love, to trust, to have mastery over your being, this is why you are here. To be in body, to learn love without condition. To learn what it feels like to hold. To forever choose the things that remove the cloak from over your heart.

Life is not fully lived, my beloved, until you have freed your heart from hiding.

A LETTER FROM THE UNIVERSE

We are in a perpetual state of growth. Our awakening and enlightenment come gradually and in concert with what we agree to face instead of turn from. The more we are willing to enter into conversation with whatever it is we confront on a daily basis, the more awake we become. And as we gradually face both big and small, we become increasingly heart minded. Arriving at this place we long for does not come from simply sitting in silence or contemplation; it comes from consciously inviting peace and acceptance to all.

With each new awakening, we gain awareness. And then we are asked to face a new situation that will bring lessons we have yet to learn. In other words, emergence is constant, and beautiful, and forever unfurling. In order for this to be a liberating thought and not a discouraging one, we must accept the perpetual shifting and unearthing with an inquisitive and nurturing heart.

We are forever learning and forever reaching for discoveries of the heart. This yielding to the inevitability of change not only gives us the strength we need when challenged, but also the strength we need to move from comfort to the uncharted and unknown. It's there where we can look for more awareness on our journey, where we can discover deeper and deeper levels of our true being-ness.

If we stay put, in whatever position we have gained in our lives, we only experience a fraction of the love available to us. Life, to me, is about being challenged to choose more love for ourselves. It's about being asked over and over again to be born into greater love. With each new corner discovered and border crossed, we can expand into new dimensions of delight. This means entering into the discomfort of our resistance again and again, harvesting each time more of who we are in truth. In blood and bone and spirit.

With each threshold reached we can push further into the unknown to experience growth and open an even larger capacity to feel our intrinsic nature. If we embody our wisdom and become heart minded, we will reap the gifts of our efforts. Love will astound and imbue us.

After you have metabolized the contents of this book, you most likely will begin to leave the concepts behind. In seeing through the eyes of our heart, the issues hidden in the body and the mind, we dissolve our attachment to these aspects of our being and are free to live without the burden of our suffering. We are free to rest as love.

Nothing written in these pages is new. These are some of the same thoughts and understandings written by the first recorded poets and sages. Rooted deep within our bodies and hearts there lives a universal language of love and kindness. This cannot leave us. Nothing is as dark as it appears, for somewhere within each of us there is a heart calling us home. We all know this, yet we continue to cycle through periods of darkness only to be saved once again by some sliver of light and hope that appears seemingly out of the blue.

You can layer fear and hate and sickness and disharmonious behaviors and thoughts on top of your heart. You can. The choice is yours. But please, if love does come to knock at your bolted doors, if some ray of gold light dances across the cold floor in front of you, if something breaks and cracks and leaves you empty, please, I pray, try to listen. Allow yourself for a moment to open to the mystery of love, to fully arrive and allow it to feed you. Drop all defenses and be nurtured. Let your starved heart be answered, soothed, and surprised by the grace at your doorstep.

PRACTICE Vow of the Heart
(Listen to this audio meditation at sarahblondin.com/heart-minded-meditations)

Here, now, in this moment, as you read these words: agree to be with yourself, with your life, to sign a new contract with your heart. You are too wise not to choose love, dear one. You are too wise to keep thinking that someone else is responsible for this life of yours.

Close your eyes, breathing into the moving constellation of your body. Reach through the churn and find your unaffected heart and presence. Take both hands and place them over your heart. Say to yourself:

I can now hear you.

I can now feel you.

I can now be you.

I will now choose you.

As long as there is life in my body, I choose you to be the breath of love that moves through me.

This is your new contract, your consciousness contract. This is the contract whereby you agree that you will actively choose yourself, your heart, your fierce undercurrent of love and liberation. You are choosing to love and care for the life in you and in another.

This is how we will reenter harmony in this world — by opening our eyes and allowing our hearts to speak and guide in all the ways it knows to. This is how we become a healthy beaming cell of life and light.

Nothing is outside of you. Your power begins the moment you choose to become the safe haven where everything in your life is welcome. No wars will be fought within or around you, for you understand that to war is to step out of your power and feed what does not nourish.

You are meant to be in love and kindness. Everything else is an obscuring of your light. It is safe here, on this planet, so long as it is safe inside you.

Be of true service, dear one, by holding your heart and becoming its faithful servant. Watch. Wait. Look. Keep eyes and heart open for life, your great wondrous life, to slowly burst from bud into a million tiny blossoms. Now. Now. Now.

You cannot unsee. If you have read this far, I am forever grateful to be sharing this journey with you. I am forever grateful for the heart that has guided you to these pages. I am forever grateful for the passageway through which we are passing together. I hope one day to meet up with your glorious frequency and light.

I bow to you, great, heart-minded warrior of love, I bow to you.

ACKNOWLEDGMENTS

Love and gratitude to my guides in the heart-minded process: Clarissa Pinkola Estés, Natalie Goldberg, John O'Donohue, Terry Tempest Williams, Hafiz, Rumi, and Mary Oliver. To all the prophets and poets and musicians who have carried me, on their backs, toward the light.

My editor, Caroline Pincus, whose gentle hand and calming support kept me steady and always made me feel seen and heard. The team at Sounds True, who trusted in me enough to help bring my work into the world.

To my firstborn, Leo, who swung the door of my heart wide open. To my youngest, Hugo, who leaks light. My mother, Julie Walsh, for her kindred spirit and unflinching love and guidance. To my dad, Normand Blondin, for his wise hands and heart, and his gift of deep listening. For my brothers David and Stephen. For David's intuitive, compassionate advice and cheerleading. And Stephen's effortless light and generosity of spirit.

My husband, Derrick Cooke, without whom this book would not be a book. Thank you for your selfless love, your grounded root and shade. Thank you for loving me every day.

For the unconditional love from my earth angel, Bree Melanson. You encourage me to come out from hiding and into the open. You lift so much weight from my shoulders. Thank you.

The friends and students of mine, who are doing the brave work of coming home to themselves. For those who shared their stories of heart opening with me—some stories are shared in this book and others inspired and informed me as I wrote. Deep gratitude to all who are doing the work with me.

And to anyone who is going through the journey of reclamation and transformation of the heart. May you find the courage and strength to continue letting go. Above all else, may you trust the light—your light.

ABOUT THE AUTHOR

Sarah Blondin is an artist and writer, and the podcast host for Live Awake. She is one of the top teachers on the popular meditation app Insight Timer, where her meditations are in constant play and have been translated into numerous languages. Her meditations are practiced by individuals all over the world and used in prisons, recovery centers, and wellness programs.

Sarah lives in Salmon Arm, British Columbia, with her husband and two sons.

More at sarahblondin.com.

ABOUT SOUNDS TRUE

SOUNDS TRUE is a multimedia publisher whose mission is to inspire and support personal transformation and spiritual awakening. Founded in 1985 and located in Boulder, Colorado, we work with many of the leading spiritual teachers, thinkers, healers, and visionary artists of our time. We strive with every title to preserve the essential "living wisdom" of the author or artist. It is our goal to create products that not only provide information to a reader or listener but also embody the quality of a wisdom transmission.

For those seeking genuine transformation, Sounds True is your trusted partner. At SoundsTrue.com you will find a wealth of free resources to support your journey, including exclusive weekly audio interviews, free downloads, interactive learning tools, and other special savings on all our titles.

To learn more, please visit SoundsTrue.com/freegifts or call us toll-free at 800.333.9185.

In loving memory of Beth Skelley, book designer extraordinaire. Her spirit lives on in our books and in our hearts.